D0423473

Saved & Depressed:

A Suicide Survivor's Journey Of Mental Health, Healing & Faith

T-Kea Blackman, MPS

Saved & Depressed: A Suicide Survivor's Journey
Of Mental Health, Healing & Faith
Copyright © 2019
ISBN: 9781096433774

All rights reserved. In accordance with the U.S. Copyright Act of 1976, the scanning, uploading, and electronic sharing of any part of this book without the permission of the publisher constitutes unlawful piracy and theft of the author's intellectual property. If you would like to use material from the book (other than for review purposes), prior written permission must be obtained by contacting T-Kea Blackman using kea@firefliesunite.com. Thank you for supporting the author's rights.

Credits
Editorial: Carla DuPont
Cover Design: Brittany Mays
Interior Design: Carla DuPont
Photography: Evvette Marcell Photography

DEDICATION

This book is dedicated to my amazing mother, Nikkita Blackman, and siblings CJ, Sabri, Khalid, Amajuwan, Amadi, and Zahiyah for being my biggest cheerleaders. Out of the many titles that I have, I am most proud to be called your daughter and big sister. Of course, I can't write this dedication and forget about the best grandma in the world, Grandma Diane; Auntie Roni and my little cousin (more like sister), Shyann. I'd also like to dedicate this book to my great grandmother, Grandma Minnie, who I've been blessed to have with me my entire life, even to this day. I don't take it lightly to have you with me. Thank you for every sacrifice you've made and for being the glue that holds our family together. I pray that my transparency and healing journey continues to inspire our family to heal and become the best version of ourselves.

To my little cousin, Nah'Jaron aka Nana, I am dedicating this book to you too. You were only 14 when you lost your life to suicide; but, I hope my advocacy makes you proud. We all love and miss you dearly.

A NOTE TO YOU

I'd like to thank you for taking the time to purchase and read my book. Your support means more to me than you will ever know. Please be prepared to experience a rollercoaster of emotions, but more importantly, I pray that reading this book encourages you to take control of your mental health and heal from the past (and maybe current) hurts.

Throughout this book, you will see that I have shared my most intimate moments with you from experiences with my family, church family, and friends. This is not to depict anyone in a negative light; it is to share my truth as I remember it and how it has impacted me. I do not place blame on anyone who I reference as I understand everyone in my circle did the best they could. While I may not be responsible for the trauma or events that took place in my life, I am responsible for my healing. This book is a part of my healing process.

Table Of Contents

Mental Health Glossary

Mental Health: How one thinks, feels, and acts determines how we handle stress, relate to others, and make choices. Mental health includes our emotional, psychological, and social well-being.

Mental Illness: A mental disorder, also called a mental illness or psychiatric disorder, is a behavioral or mental pattern that causes significant distress or impairment of personal functioning. Mental disorders are usually defined by a combination of how a person behaves, feels, perceives, or thinks. (E.g. bipolar disorder, major depressive disorder, post-traumatic stress disorder, etc.)

Psychologist: One who has a doctorate in psychology; either a Ph.D. or a Psy.D and completes evaluations.

Psychiatrist: A type of physician; one who attended medical school then did a four-year residency in psychiatry, a medical specialty focusing on mind-body interactions and mental disorders. Psychiatrist can prescribe medications.

Psychiatric NP: Nurse-practitioners can assess, evaluate and prescribe medications.

Therapist: Can be a psychiatrist, psychologist, or master's level professional trained in mental health, behavioral health and psychology.

Masters level professionals are licensed in Marriage & Family Therapy (LMFT), Clinical Social Work (LCSW), Professional Counseling (LCPC), and other disciplines.

Each of the above professionals has a different and distinct way of training and length of time spent in training. Typically, psychiatrists and psychologists spend the most years in training and/or research. Psychologists are usually extensively trained in psychotherapy. Psychiatrists are trained in psychotherapy and in medical and mental health disorders.

Psychotropic Medication: A licensed psycho-active drug taken to exert an effect on the chemical makeup of the brain and nervous system; medications that are used to treat mental illnesses.

Recovery: A process of change through which individuals improve their health and wellness, live a self-directed life, and strive to reach their full potential, according to the Substance Abuse and Mental Health Administration.

Saved & Depressed:

A Suicide Survivor's Journey Of Mental Health, Healing & Faith

Chapter ONE

It Would Be Better If I Was Dead

It would be better if I wasn't alive, was the text message I sent to a friend. An hour later, I was awakened by two policemen breaking into my window and yelling into my apartment. They asked if I could make it to the door to let them in. I told them I would try and it seemed like it took me 20 minutes to make it to the door. My body was weak from not having anything to drink or eat in three days.

After opening the door, the police officers asked me if I was okay. I told them I wasn't too sure. They asked me when was the last time I had eaten and if I wanted to hurt myself. I told them I had already tried and it didn't work. I described how I took a countless number of pills and drank a bottle of wine, planning not to wake up. At that point, the police officers stated that I was a threat to myself and must be taken to the hospital, but I had two options. Option one was to handcuff me so they could transport me; option two was to call the paramedics to have them transport me. I agreed to be transported by the paramedics.

Upon arriving at the hospital, I was evaluated by the psychiatrist who told me that I also had two options. *What's up with everyone giving me two options? And neither option giving me a choice of doing what I wanted to do which was to die.* Option one: I could voluntarily check myself into the hospital. Option two: I would be involuntarily checked into the hospital. I did not understand the difference as both options seemed the same.

He told me that by checking myself in, it would give me more control of the process. After I agreed to check myself in, the nurse came and asked me to remove all my belongings. She also took my cell phone. A few hours later, my worst nightmare came true; I was transported to the psychiatric unit. As soon as the doors opened, I noticed people in the common area who I was immediately afraid of. The only image I had in my head about the psychiatric unit was from one of my favorite childhood movies *Good Burger*. You know what I am talking about, right? The "zombie looking" people in straight-jackets. So the fact that I was in the place where "crazy people" went to be tamed did not make sense to me.

The doors locked from the inside and outside. I was rolled into a room to have my vitals taken by a nurse and cried like a baby. I had never been so scared in my life as I was on that day. I walked into my room and noticed white walls, a locked and blurred out window, and a girl in the other bed sleeping. I laid in the bed and cried myself to sleep.

The next morning, I was awakened by a psychiatrist who asked me about my suicide attempt. He wanted details like if I had heard voices. He told me they would put me on medication to help with my uncontrollable suicidal thoughts. Moments later, one of the technicians told me that breakfast was ready and it could not be eaten in the room; only in the common area. Even though my stomach was growling with pain from not eating in four days, I refused to go into the common area with "those people." I asked to call my family. When my mom didn't answer, I called my aunt. I remember her words like it was yesterday, "Kea, you do not belong there with those people." I did not think so either, but apparently the police and doctors disagreed.

I went back into my room refusing to eat. When the social worker tried to talk to me, I became angry, threw the papers down, and refused her help. By day two I was ready to go home. Being in the unit brought on feelings of hate because it felt like a jail. I had to ask to take showers, make phone calls, and fed three meals and two snacks per day. While lying in my bed, I asked myself questions like, *How did I get here? How does someone with an apartment, a car, two degrees, and a promising career end up in the place that I was told is for "crazy people"?*

I finally decided to walk out of the room to eat breakfast. One of the staff members walked over to talk to me. She asked me how I was doing, I told her I didn't belong there. She asked me to explain further. My exact words were, "I have a bachelor's from Howard University and a master's from Georgetown University. People like me do not belong here." She looked at me then responded, "Highly educated people get sick too. You are here because you are sick. Your brain is an organ just like your heart. If you do not take care of it, it will become sick. You are here to get better."

For some reason when she said those words, they stuck with me. I started to accept that I did belong there. I asked for the social worker because I wanted to go home. The social worker told me the only way I could go home was if I agreed to try group therapy and participated in the Partial Hospitalization Program (PHP), a comprehensive, short-term outpatient option that provides support and treatment for adults facing mental and/or substance abuse disorders. Agreeing to this method of treatment allowed me to go home the next day. I called friends to come pick me up. Shout out to Bria and Chi Chi (my Howard sisters). Little did I know that my recovery was just beginning. I stayed at the hospital six hours a day for PHP, but I was able to go home at night. Thank God!

PHP was filled with individual and group therapy. I was assigned a therapist and psychiatrist who monitored me while I was on a new mediation. I met some of the most amazing people and looked forward to attending every day because it was a safe, stigma free zone. I did not have to worry about being called crazy or dramatic, or people saying things like, "Girl, ain't nothing wrong with you," or "What do you have to be depressed about?" I could simply be and express my thoughts and feelings without the fear of being judged by others. During group sessions, we discussed topics such as building a support system, setting boundaries and anger management. It was the beginning of healing from watching my mom be verbally and physically abused by my siblings' dad (not to be referred to as my step-dad) and the absence of my father due to drug abuse and incarceration.

A few months after I was discharged from the hospital, I told my paternal grandfather what happened and he said, "Oh, when I was 14-years-old I attempted suicide. We recently committed my brother, your great-uncle, to the psychiatric unit because he struggles with schizophrenia." Immediately, I thought to myself, *Why wasn't this something that was shared with me while growing up?* Of course, stigma played a huge role and during that time mental health was swept under the rug. In many cases it was "prayed away."

When adults spoke to me, it was always about going to college, staying involved in extracurricular activities, having a successful career and drilling 'no sex' in my head. Talking about mental health should have been no different. Did you know that a specific gene is linked to suicidal behavior? A study by the Centre for Addiction and Mental Health found evidence that a specific gene is linked to suicidal behavior. The study included data from 3,352 people and 1,202 of them had a history of suicidal behavior.[1] This means mental illness and suicide are genetic for some families. About 90% of people who die by suicide have at least one mental health disorder such as schizophrenia, depression, bipolar disorder, or general mood disorder.[2] It is also important to consider environmental risk factors such as early childhood or recent trauma and the use of addictive drugs or medications along with other factors. This is important because many tend to view suicide as a weakness, a selfish act or lack of faith in God. Wait a minute, I'll get to the church in the next few chapters. The reality is, people with mental illness

---

[1] Science Daily:
https://www.sciencedaily.com/releases/2011/10/111007113941.htm
[2] National Alliance On Mental Illness:
https://www.nami.org/learn-more/mental-health-by-the-numbers

are sick. Think of it this way, if we don't take care of bodies, they become sick and the same for our brains.

Before my diagnoses, I limited mental illness to the man or woman walking down the street talking to themselves and people who were out of touch with reality. Now I know there are levels to this! There is a spectrum and there is no token person for the face of mental illness. Your doctor or teacher may have a mental illness and you would never know. Prior to my diagnoses of major depressive and generalized anxiety disorders, I thought I was simply experiencing moments of sadness here and there. It was not until my suicidal thoughts became uncontrollable and I stopped being able to do daily living activities like cooking, cleaning, and working that I realized this was more than just sadness.

Suicidal thoughts weren't new for me. I started having thoughts about dying and ending my life at 12-years-old. As I became older, they became progressively worse. I would think about driving my car into a divider or another car so it would look like an accident instead of a suicide. My body ached from head to toe. I felt paralyzed and as if I had a ton of bricks on top of me. Therefore, pushing the bricks off was impossible. My mind would race so bad to the point one of my legs would shake without stopping. I could not concentrate; I called out of work at least three times a week. During this time, I worked as a receptionist and people began to talk about me in the office saying I looked sick and was absent in the face. I was not completing assignments; instead I was missing deadlines and was frequently tardy. Simply put, I hated life and wanted to die.

I was in graduate school and God's grace was the only way I made it through because I was hanging on by a thread. I was living paycheck to paycheck, so my bills were often paid late and my credit score dropped significantly. I lost my uncle and a close friend of my family to physical illnesses. Shortly after those deaths, my younger cousin died by suicide. Suicide began to seem like the best option to escape the emotional and mental pain.

Chapter TWO

Depression Is Not A Synonym For Sadness

I remember having a conversation with a friend explaining the physically and mentally crippling effects of my depression. After processing the conversation, it made me realize that not only was it hard to explain what my lows were like, but it was a challenge for some to understand. I left the conversation feeling misunderstood as if I chose to stay in bed, not eat, and have suicidal thoughts. Translation, "Kea, you're being lazy."

The interesting part is how, as humans, we like to naturally compare our experiences as a way to connect with one another. While that can be helpful and make us feel like we are not dealing with life's challenges on our own, the damaging part is that it can easily discredit another's experience. My friend stated that as a parent, staying in bed is not an option and pushing through is a must for the children. Here is why that statement can be troubling for me and others who struggle with depression. While my friend did not state that I was being lazy, the comparison made me feel as if I was. We all have days where we don't feel like going to work, school, cooking, etc., but that feeling should not be confused with someone who is battling depression. I do not have the ability to "push through" when I am in an episode. That ability is gone. It is nonexistent. I often hear people say "push through." Don't you think if I could push through, I would?

In fact, the medication helps me to do simple things like shower and eat. A therapist told me that she worked with a client who would urinate in water bottles and leave them in the closet of his bedroom. While that may not make sense to someone who's never been severely depressed, I certainly understand it. We are so quick to judge someone and think just because we can do something, someone else should be able to do it, too.

With depression, there is a persistent lack of energy and motivation even though I wholeheartedly want to do things such as record my podcast and hang out with family and friends. However, it is physically impossible to move. In fact, there are days when I don't feel like doing anything and I make myself to get up and get things done. In those instances, I am usually tired or need a "lazy day," but I'm not in a depression. Others with depression have lost the meaning to live life and would rather die. I have been there too. This should never be confused with *choosing* to be crippled by the illness or being lazy.

Depression is the leading disability worldwide.[3] Yes, it is a disability and should be

---

[3] World Health Organization: https://www.who.int/news-room/fact-sheets/detail/depression

treated as such. Would you say to a cancer patient that they are choosing to lose hair and become progressively weak? While that may seem far-fetched, it is the same thing with depression. I don't choose not to complete daily activities or take care of my hygiene; I am simply unable to. Please think twice before comparing your struggles with someone else's. Hear what the person is saying instead of comparing and potentially, minimizing their experiences.

For some reason, many people think that a person who struggles with depression is sitting at home crying; or maybe it's like the movies where the person is sitting on the couch watching TV and eating a bowl of ice cream; or better yet, the person is looking out of a window and it's raining outside to further imply how the person is feeling. I'm very hesitant when a person says that they are depressed because it is a serious illness and should be treated as such.

As I stated before, there are levels to this and I'm referring to those of us who have been paralyzed by this illness. Sometimes I think people are actually sad and can't differentiate the two. While I do not believe in discrediting the way anyone feels because it has been done to me on numerous occasions, I want people to truly understand depression versus experiencing sadness, which is a common emotion. While there is some gray area between the two, there is a clear difference.

Let's start with sadness. Sadness is a common human emotion. It might be triggered by an event that is hurtful, shocking, or challenging — such as a breakup. But when something good happens, the sadness fades away. For example, your significant other leaves for an extended period of time on a work assignment or your car breaks down and you don't have the money to pay for it. Either one of these situations has the potential to make you sad. You're human. It's normal to feel sad when life happens. Once you get the money to repair your car or your significant other returns home, you find that you bounce back easily. My point is that an event or experience happened to trigger your sadness and once the experience has changed for the better, your sadness faded away.

So what is the difference between sadness and depression? A person who struggles with depression can certainly experience sadness, but it is more than just the blues. An event might trigger the depression, such as the loss of a job that leaves you unable to take care of yourself or your family. The difference is, a person can get a new job and still be depressed. Or maybe it's been six months after your loved one has passed and no matter what you do, you can't shake the feeling. That's why saying things like, "Just snap out of it," or "Some people have it worse than you," is irrelevant. To be honest, it is also insensitive and minimizes the illness.

Asking a person why they are depressed is not always the best approach because sometimes people don't know why they are depressed. A person struggling with depression cannot turn it on or off. Depression is an emotional state and it affects your perception, thoughts and behaviors.[4] Unlike sadness, depression does not always require an event to happen for a depressive episode to be triggered. In fact, I have found many cases where people appear to be fine "on paper" because they have the American dream of financial stability, good education, and a beautiful family in a nice home. Yet, they are still depressed. For example, Robin Williams and Marilyn Monroe lost their lives to suicide. From the outside looking in, the Hollywood life seems like they have it all from money, to fame to material possessions. That's why I want to reiterate saying things like, "You have nothing to be depressed about," is one of the most insensitive things you can say to someone. Instead, offer a listening ear, validate their

---

[4] National Institute of Mental Health:
https://www.nimh.nih.gov/health/topics/depression/index.sht ml

feelings, encourage mental health treatment, and provide support, if you can.

The cause of depression is unknown, but trauma, genetics, life circumstances, drug or alcohol abuse, medical conditions, and brain changes trigger the illness. For some, depression might be a lifelong chronic illness, while others might only experience it once in their life. For many, it requires treatment such as therapy and medication. There are many symptoms listed in the Diagnostic and Statistical Manual of Mental Disorders (DSM), the severity of which can vary from person to person. The DSM is basically the bible of mental health diagnoses. Here is a list of some of the symptoms of depression that must last for at least two weeks:

> Sleeping too much or too little
> Rapid weight loss or weight gain
> A change in appetite
> Fatigue
> Slowed down movements or feeling restless most days
> Feeling tired, sluggish, or like you have no energy
> Having suicidal thoughts
> Having a hard time concentrating and making decisions
> A loss or decrease in interest in activities that you usually enjoy

> Feelings of worthlessness or excessive guilt and isolation

Here are some questions I would ask myself to check if I'm struggling with depression:

> Are my sleeping and eating routine the same or did they change?
> Do I still enjoy the things that make me happy?
> Are my emotions triggered by a specific event? If the event changes for the better, does my mood get better?
> Have I had thoughts about harming myself?
> Do I have difficulty concentrating?
> Have I had a loss of energy for no specific reason?
> Am I taking care of my hygiene?
> Am I having a hard time getting out of bed?

I hope this helps you understand the difference between sadness and depression and begin to become more cautious before using the word "depressed." If you're reading this and struggling with depression, please consider seeking medical treatment. There is help and you are not alone.

Chapter THREE

A Trip Down Memory Lane

Being raised in Elizabeth, New Jersey in public housing, I remember seeing crack bottles and urine in the hallways and elevator of my building. Drug dealers and people who were addicted to drugs were common. As a child, I never thought I was poor for the following reasons:

> ➢ I came home to a clean house with food on the table and had clean clothes and shoes.
> ➢ My mom worked and gave me almost everything I wanted.
> ➢ I was surrounded by family and friends who loved me.

When most people think about the projects, they tend to think of images like those from the TV show *The Wire*. Unkept children, empty refrigerators, dirty homes, you name it. Let me say this, before someone who really knows me jumps down my throat about my childhood, *The Wire* is a far stretch from where I grew up. There were similarities, like low income public housing a.k.a. the projects/hood, violence, drugs, teenage pregnancy, and a lot of people on government assistance.

Many of the people I know on government assistance have no desire of getting off as it is a way of life. It is a continued cycle of poverty. For instance, a girl who grows up in the projects will become a teen mom, collect government assistance, and move out of her mom's apartment to get an apartment in the same public assistance apartment complex. This isn't an issue isolated to my hood, but hoods across the country.

In fact, my father was a drug dealer and user. I used to be so embarrassed and did not want my dad coming to any of my dance shows, pageants or doctor's appointments. I was a daddy's girl. After unfilled promises and visiting him in jail countless times, my heart was broken. I felt like my dad chose his drugs over me. I remember walking in my parents' bedroom when I was 6-years-old and seeing a bag of drugs on the bed. I walked in on my dad, on numerous occasions, nodding off with a bag of drugs sitting next to him on the bed. Those images are glued in my brain, something that I will never forget. I watched my dad's mom struggle with drug addiction and remember throughout my childhood seeing her look sick. Through my recovery, I understand that addiction is a disease and my dad and grandmother were sick.

The absence of my dad left me with trust and abandonment issues that I did not realize until I was in my early twenties. I thought because I wasn't promiscuous and made it past becoming a teen mom, I turned out well. Little did I know that it would show up differently for me. I struggled with attachment issues, sacrificing myself, like having sex for the first time with my ex-boyfriend even though I was not ready, because I thought it would keep him around. It did not work because he still broke up with me two days after. News flash! You cannot keep someone who does not want to be kept.

After my parents separated, my mom started dating another guy who she eventually had five children with. At the age of 12, I saw him hit my mom and it shattered my world. I remember being scared. It was hard to like him because of the verbal and physical abuse. He threatened to kill my mom and was destructive. One time, he took our desktop and threw it out of the window. He allegedly put sugar in my mom's gas tank. No one saw him do it, but the mechanic told my mom she had sugar in her gas tank. Since he has a history of destroying things, I assumed it was him. He stole her car, money and degraded her. I remember a time when he grabbed the steering wheel while my mom was driving and made her swerve into oncoming traffic. There were times I called the police and when they arrived, my mom said that everything was okay.

That environment created a lot of anxiety for me because I never knew when an incident would occur. They were sporadic. They could fight one day and another incident may not happen for another six months. There were times when they would break up and he would leave. Talk about happiness... then he would come back.

I remember one night, I woke up in the middle of the night and left my room to sleep with my mom. When I walked in her bedroom, I saw that he was there and turned around to go back into my room and started crying. My grandma heard me and asked, "What's wrong, Kea?" I said, "He's back."

As a way to keep myself safe and avoid feeling sad and scared when he was in the house, I was involved in Girls Scouts, a drill team, dance, my school's band, community fashion shows, choir, and theatre. I even went to school early to receive extra help and did not come home until after my extracurricular activities. I did this so when I got home, I just had to do my homework, take a shower and go to bed. Then there were moments when a fight would break out and I had a difficult time finishing my homework. As a teenager, I became angry with mom because I did not understand why she put our family through this hell. There was a season when my mom and I argued a lot because I resented her for taking him back repeatedly.

She became upset that I was "telling her business" to my church family. I was not sharing it to put her in a negative light, but talking about my experiences as a way to release the emotions I was experiencing. During an argument, I ran away and started having thoughts of suicide. I only went around the corner to a friend's house, but my mom didn't know that. Honestly, almost every time my mom and siblings' dad got into an argument, I would feel suicidal. This would never escape my lips as a child. I did not know what the word suicide meant. I just knew I wanted to die and contemplated how to end my life on numerous occasions. My high school guidance counselor provided me with an outlet to vent and pushed me academically. I contribute my ability to push through high school to him. Thanks, Mr. O.! Did you know…

> large amounts of stress causes damage to the temporal lobe of the brain in children who will suffer severe emotional and cognitive problems, have difficulty in making and/or sustaining positive relationships?[5]

> children who grow up with domestic violence are 6 times more likely to die by suicide and 50% more likely to abuse drugs and alcohol?[6] As you can see, my childhood trauma has a direct correlation to my anxiety and depression disorders and suicide attempt.

---

[5] Childhood Domestic Violence Association:
https://cdv.org/2014/02/10-startling-domestic-violence-statistics-for-children/
[6] Ibid

- ➢ children who come from violent homes are more likely to experience psychological problems short and long-term?[7]
- ➢ children who've experienced domestic violence often meet the diagnostic criteria for post-traumatic stress disorder (PTSD) and the effects on their brains are similar to those experienced by combat veterans?[8]
- ➢ living with domestic violence significantly alters a child's DNA, aging them prematurely 7-10 years?[9]
- ➢ children who grow up with domestic violence are 74% more likely to commit a violent crime against someone else?[10]
- ➢ children of domestic violence are 3 times more likely to repeat the cycle in adulthood
- ➢ growing up with domestic violence is the most significant predictor of whether or not someone will be engaged in domestic violence later in life?[11]

Trauma plays a major role in mental health disorders, how one perceives the world and

---

[7] Ibid
[8] Ibid
[9] Ibid
[10] Ibid
[11] Ibid

responds to life events whether we realize it or not. Prior to my diagnoses, I thought it was normal to walk around on edge all of the time. I had no clue that being "worked up" and worried 24/7 was a problem. In fact, I thought everyone struggled with uncontrollable and racing thoughts to the point where they could not focus, sleep, or get daily activities completed until one day my therapist suggested medication which I was completely against. When I was in PHP, the psychiatrist gave me medication for my anxiety and within a couple of hours, I was calm. I was like, "Oh this what it feels like not to be on edge. This is freaking amazing!"

Chapter FOUR

Stuntin' For The Gram

Erica just got engaged. *"Oh, that's just great, another person is getting married."* Marcus just got a promotion. *"I guess I am happy for him."* Brittany got a new job with a salary increase and she's expecting her first child. Rachel is traveling to Italy. Another black person killed by a police officer. *"So you mean to tell me another one of my childhood friends was shot and killed?"*

A few months after getting my diagnosis, these were the thoughts that ran through my mind constantly as I scrolled down my news feed on Facebook. I would sweat and my mind would swirl with a mixture of emotions. I began to ask myself question after question. "What can I do to protect my brothers against police brutality in this country? What can I do in my community to help? Why does everything appear to be so perfect in everyone else's life? Is something wrong with me? Why is their life moving and mine isn't?"

Of course, I know what I see on social media is only a small portion of someone's everyday life. Most people only share good news with the exception of the senseless killings in my community and the world. So yes, I know there is such a thing as a filter on social media. People filter what they post to make themselves be seen in the best light. I used to have my filter as well on social media, but that didn't change the fact that I used to compare myself to my peers and discredit all my accomplishments. This empty feeling would overwhelm me for a moment, then I would become angry. I wish it was only an occasional inconvenience, but I found myself feeling this way multiple times a day on social media.

So, you may ask, "How many hours did you spend on social media?" Honestly, I have no idea, but I used to scroll through my feed at work, at home on the couch, in church, when I was hanging out with friends, and in the middle of the night when I woke up. I enjoyed posting selfies, sharing the highlights of my life, encouraging others through words of affirmation, and scrolling through my news feed to see what was going on in the world and among my peers. Most importantly, I used it to escape my depression, although it also contributed to my depression and anxiety. Talk about a double-edged sword. In the moment, I would feel fine. Once I got off social media, I continued to compare myself. And like so many of us, I sought validation from likes, comments, and followers.

After being off of social media for five months, I noticed I did not have the desire to go back on it. I finally decided to get on Facebook and the empty feeling did not come back. Maybe because I could not get myself to scroll through my news feed. When I logged onto Facebook, I immediately clicked my profile and checked my notifications. Three days later, I deactivated my account because I knew I was not ready. Considering that I attempted suicide the month before, I had to be honest with myself by admitting that I was not mentally strong enough. Then I immediately asked myself, *Would I ever be?*

As I began to do some research on major depressive disorder and social media, I discovered an article on EverydayHealth.com. In this piece, psychologist Stephanie Mihalas, PHD, says spending too much time on social media can create a negative cycle of thoughts, and social media can actually become a root for unhealthy emotions because of that. In addition, Natascha M. Santos, PsyD, says it can lead you to process information with a negative bias and have dysfunctional beliefs. It can even cause you to minimize the positives of your own relationships by comparing them to others. Photos posted and status updates are carefully crafted, yet still often put a depressed person in a place where he/she begins to compare his or her entire life to someone else's highlights. I said to myself, *"Yes, that is me!"*

Four years later, I am in a place where those emotions do not come up for me. One of my friends is struggling with comparison and she asked me how I was able to work through it. I said, "Shout-out to therapy and a year of being off of social media." I told her if I begin to compare myself to someone's social media post(s), I ask myself, "What emotion(s) am I experiencing?" and "Why am I feeling this way?" In my early twenties, I used to feel the need to share everything amazing happening in my life. For instance, I would post pictures of myself working backstage at BET's Black Girls Rock! or meeting a celebrity.

Looking back, I realized that I was only covering up the anxiety and depression that I was experiencing. I was not diagnosed during that time, but I see how I was caught up in keeping a facade online. So many people believed the happiness I portrayed. I even fooled myself. That is the reason why when I informed people of my suicide attempt, I received responses like, "You seem so happy and like you have life figured out," or "What do you have to be depressed about? You have a college degree." As if somehow my college degrees and accomplishments could stop the suicidal thoughts and the pain I was feeling.

I also put myself on this unrealistic timeline like many of my peers. Didn't you set an unrealistic timeline for yourself? The one that says, by the time I am 25-years-old, I will have my dream job. By the time I am 30-years-old, I will be happily married living in my big house inside of a white picket fence playing with my beautiful children. Those pressures may come from ourselves, parents and/or society. We are told when we graduate from college, we are supposed to get a "good job" and start a family. But what happens when you do not meet the timeline you set out for yourself? You are left feeling disappointed or like a failure. Society has changed and it is rare for things to pan out in this order: Graduate college, obtain dream job, get married, have children, and retire.

Once I realized this, I started to redefine success for myself. I no longer limit the success I can reach to being married, having children, and developing a great career. What good is the big house, money, marriage, children, and a great career if you are unhappy? Why is it that we associate material things with happiness? In fact, so many of us buy things to cover up our insecurities and fill voids. My desire for children seems to dissipate the older I become and the more I learn about myself. I thought as a woman I was supposed to be a mother; that was the only reason I wanted children. The beautiful thing is that I am young and can change my mind about motherhood in the future. However, I do not compare myself to another woman who may have that desire. We all have different values and one woman valuing her career over being a mother does not make one better than the other. Some women want both and that's okay too!

If I did not take the time to step away from social media, work on myself in therapy and define success for myself, I would still be posting pictures and trying to convince myself and others that I am happy. It is one of the reasons I believe in being so transparent, as it is rare to find people being authentic and vulnerable online. We live in a time where people are renting private planes and Louis Vuitton bags to post them on social media. Remember the #BowWowChallenge? If you don't know what it is, please do yourself a favor and Google it. People are creating new identities that are unfortunately feeding their insecurities, depression, and anxiety. Therefore, it is not far-fetched to say that some people are not "living their best life" on social media; they are "living their best lie." Maybe that's a question to ask yourself…what are you living?

Chapter FIVE

Breaking Generational Curses &
The Loman Family Lynching

Like many black families, I cannot trace my family's history past my maternal great-great-grandma. Even being able to go back that far is a blessing as some can't trace their history past their grandparents. I've been fortunate to know both sets of my grandparents and three sets of my great-grandparents. Again, like many black families, not all information is passed down and as a way to "deal", we swept things under the rug or "prayed it away." So, it shouldn't have been a surprise when I discovered that my great-great-grandmother's family was set up by the Klu Klux Klan (KKK) and the National Association for the Advancement of Colored People (NAACP) became involved. It became a national case that shifted the way cases were handled during the Reconstruction Era. Brace yourself because this story sounds like something out of a movie.

Clarence, Demon, and Bertha Lowman were accused of murdering Sheriff Henry Hampton of Aiken County, South Carolina. The sheriff and two of his deputies entered the Lowman family (my family) home because they were accused of illegally selling liquor. The police officers did not have on uniforms or badges when they arrived at the home. Bertha Lowman and her mother, Annie, were home with other family members, including my great-great-grandmother, Elenora Lowman. Annie asked her daughter to go inside of the house and when Bertha turned to go inside, the officers ran toward the women. Sheriff Howard hit Bertha in the mouth with his gun. Annie picked up an ax and was about to hit Sheriff Howard to defend her daughter. Sadly, she was shot and killed by the deputies before she could help her daughter. Demon and Clarence Lowman, Annie's son and nephew began shooting at the officers. The sheriff was killed and Bertha was wounded.

Bertha, Demon, and Clarence were charged with the death of the sheriff. Annie's husband, Sam, was sent to jail for allegedly possessing illegal alcohol. Demon and Clarence received the death penalty, and Bertha was given a life sentence in jail. Sam was found not guilty on October 8, 1926 after a retrial. News of the trial spread like wildfire and the case went to the Supreme Court. Former NAACP Executive Secretary Walter White was a catalyst for lynching cases and could pass as being white with his pale skin, blondish hair, and blue eyes. He helped to investigate my family's case by going to South Carolina as a reporter. White infiltrated the KKK and was able to discover information to support the case. They were convicted; but, the Supreme Court overturned the convictions and ordered new trials because the officers entered the home without a warrant.

During the retrials, an angry mob of approximately 30 to 40 people went into the jail where my family members were held and transported them to a pine forest north of town. Clarence was able to escape by jumping from the car he was held in. He was then shot, recaptured and dragged by a rope behind a car to be lynched. The mob stated that Bertha was the hardest to kill as she dragged herself over the ground and begged for her life. She was shot a number of times before they killed her. Unfortunately, no one was ever indicted in connection with the lynching. I'm sure you're not surprised. Years later, similar cases emerged of blacks being killed such as Emmett Till, Trayvon Martin, and Mike Brown, where officers or white men were not convicted of the crime they clearly committed.

According to White and an NAACP press release regarding the Lowman family, the following was concluded:

1. The lynching was planned and executed by members of the KKK.
2. Officers of the law took part in the lynching and a number of them acted as unofficial executioners of the mob victims.
3. The prisoners were turned over to the mob by the sheriff and his assistants.

4. Reputable white citizens living in the vicinity were in terror of their lives from the lawless KKK ring and went heavily armed, barred their doors at night, and had been "praying to God" for some person from outside of the state to come in and bare the facts.

5. Within one hour after the judge's decision, news had been sent as far away as Columbia that the three Lowmans were to be lynched that night. Within the same hour, the KKK held a meeting in the office of a prominent white attorney of Aiken County, South Carolina, who had been recently elected to the State Legislature.

I have not been to Aiken County, South Carolina but I plan to visit to gather information on my family's history. According to my great-great aunt, one of the trees where my family members were lynched is still standing in South Carolina today.

Generational Trauma & Mental Health

The torture of my family members brings great heartache, as well as discovering the notion that I would not be here today if my great-great-grandmother, Elenora Lowman, did not escape from the home. I am a direct descendant of her, therefore, my great-grandmother, who I am so fortunate to still have, my grandmother, nor my mother would have existed. You may be asking what this has to do with mental health. It has everything to do with mental health as trauma is often passed on when it is not addressed.

We've heard the saying, "what happens in this house stays in this house." This is the kind of thinking that allows family members who sexually abuse children to continue to come around and act as if everything is normal. As a result, when children become adults, they often have a negative way of viewing the world, build emotional walls, are broken, lack trust, suppress their hurt, and turn to unhealthy ways of coping such as drugs and alcohol. The sad part is trauma damages us so much that we don't even realize we are broken and it becomes normalized.

Intergenerational trauma is not limited to what happened in the past as it has a direct correlation to the current generation and it will happen for future generations if the trauma is never addressed. According to "What Generational Trauma Looks Like" an article by The Huffington Post, children of Holocaust survivors have lower levels of cortisol, a hormone that helps humans manage stress, making them less able to handle stressful situations. They also have been found to have higher rates of cardiovascular disease, high blood pressure, and other chronic illnesses, such as diabetes and fibromyalgia. This can be applied to trauma from slavery, segregation, and any other traumatic events.

No one in my family mentioned this story to me, not even my great-grandmother, and her mother was in the home when the incident occurred. It was not until my great-aunt discovered a genealogy show and realized that it was our family story being told on TV.

Let's define trauma first. Trauma is an emotional wound that causes intense stress to the brain. As a result, it impacts the chemicals in your brain, the way you behave, respond, and think after the trauma that has taken place. Trauma varies in intensity depending on the situation, it can be anything from slavery, to a car accident, to sexual abuse, to divorce, to the death of a loved one, or experiencing homelessness. In my case, we are referring to intergenerational trauma, which is caused by events that target a group of people. In fact, even though I was not born during the tragedy of my family members, research shows that even family members who have not directly experienced the trauma can feel the effects of the event(s) generations later (e.g. Slave Trade, September 11th, and the Holocaust). When children are exposed to trauma and experience higher levels of stress as their brains are developing, the trauma damages the temporal lobe of the brain. As a result, children suffer severe emotional and cognitive problems, as well as have difficulty in making and/or sustaining positive relationships, according to research by the Center For Disease Control and Prevention. Children who experience trauma often operate in fight-flight-freeze mode even when there is no danger present. Fight-flight-freeze is a psychological reaction that happens when you're in danger and your body is trying to protect you. For instance, it can be as simple as sweating and a racing heart due to a fear of public speaking, to something more severe like running away from a sexual predator. According to The Study for Child and Adolescent Mental Health, intergenerational trauma can negatively impact families as a result of the following[12]

- ➢ Unresolved emotions and thoughts about a traumatic event
- ➢ Repeated patterns of negative behavior including beliefs about parenting
- ➢ Untreated or poorly treated substance abuse or severe mental illness
- ➢ Poor parent-child relationships and emotional attachment

---

[12] National Institute of Mental Health:
https://www.nimh.nih.gov/health/topics/child-and-adolescent-mental-health/index.shtml

- ➢ Complicated personality traits or personality disorders
- ➢ Content attitude about the way things are within the family

This brings me to the recent studies of epigenetics[13]. Studies are still taking place to further prove epigenetics. Epigenetics is the study of biological mechanisms that switch genes on and off. We know that DNA comes from our parents such as hair and eye color, but epigenetics is the passing of the way the genes are used. In simple terms, epigenetics has the ability to impact and alter specific genes in your DNA. What you eat, where live, how you age, life experiences, your social circle, and how you exercise can all eventually cause chemical modifications around the genes that have the ability to impact and alter specific genes in your DNA. Research reveals that you have the ability to potentially turn the genes that are detrimental to your health on and off.

Let's take my great-great-grandmother who was never treated for the trauma of watching the murder of multiple loved ones take place, having to escape, and almost losing her life. I was told by my great-aunt that her mother (my great-great-grandmother) never talked about what took place

---

[13] What Is Epigenetics?: https://www.whatisepigenetics.com/what-is-epigenetics/

during her childhood. I assume it was something that she tried to forget. As a result, she suppressed her thoughts and emotions which increased her chances of developing post-traumatic stress disorder (PTSD), depression, and anxiety. I can't say exactly how the trauma impacted her, but based on the research of intergenerational trauma and epigenetics, this event possibly altered genes in her DNA that were subsequently passed down to my great-grandmother, who passed it down to my grandmother, who passed it down to my mother, who passed it down to me. In addition, my mother was also diagnosed with major depressive disorder and PTSD. Part of her diagnosis is based on her current trauma, but I wonder how much of it was passed down from down our Lowman family members.

Of course, mental health treatment, science, technology, and education were not nearly as advanced as they are today, and as a black woman, she would not have received treatment anyway. During that time, all she had was prayer and whatever she thought was best to deal with the trauma. I share my family's history because I want you to understand that traumatic events have the power, not only to change how your genes are used, but how you think and respond to the world around you.

Imagine having cancer and not being treated for 10 plus years. Would you die? The same goes for trauma, as many of us are walking around feeling numb and dead because of traumatic events and generational trauma. It is my hope that after reading this chapter, you practice compassion toward yourself and others, in addition to receiving mental health treatment when tragic events occur in your life.

When I first started sharing my story via articles, events, and my podcast, my mom was uncomfortable and 'til this day, she has a difficult time listening to my podcast as it presents challenges that she is currently working through. I explained to my mom that my intention is not to air our family's dirty laundry or present her in a negative light. I am sharing my story and she happens to be a part of my story. Sharing my story is a part of my healing process because suppressing it fed the depression, anxiety, and suicidal thoughts; it was killing me. My prayer is that I continue to have a ripple effect on my family and community.

I asked my family to share how my mental health recovery has impacted them and here's what they had to say:

"Your journey has forced me to look at myself and realize I was struggling with depression. I look at

mental health from a different perspective. I am now in therapy and realize I am in an unhealthy relationship." - **Mommy**

"The suicide attempt of my sister taught me that every person you love must be cherished as if you'll never see them again. The fact that a person can tell you that they're alright and not be is now always in my conscience when conversing with any individual. I learned that the world can be deceiving and people can be misleading, and that you can never assume you know anything about someone based on their possessions. With the tremendous amount of suicides, it is critical to spread positivity and love as much as possible, for it can be the ultimate factor if a person is under the belief that their death should be chosen over their life." - **Sabri (brother)**

"T-Kea's journey is an example of never judge a book by its cover. It ultimately helped me and so many others have the opportunity to get a better understanding of how unbiased mental illness is and how it can affect anyone. When you look at a successful person, it is very easy to believe that a person cannot suffer from a mental illness. Now with T-Kea sharing her story, I know that accolades cannot cure or keep away mental illness. By talking about mental illness, it begins to create an atmosphere that is educational and

gives people a better understanding of mental illness." - **Grandma Diane**

"T-Kea has accomplished so much in her life. I have always admired her as being a beautiful, strong, motivated young lady. I did not know that she was going through so much mental pain. I never knew that someone who seemed so happy and devotes her life to inspiring others was also dying on the inside. But her struggle, her journey, and her perseverance are now more admiring to me than anything she has ever done. She has taught me that mental illness can affect any race, gender, rich or poor person. She has also taught me that there is nothing wrong with seeking help; it doesn't mean that you are crazy." - **Auntie Roni**

"T-Kea's mental health journey was extremely educational and important to my understanding of mental health. Mental illness is very relevant in today's society because it's something that affects such a large population. Her journey simply broadened my knowledge and helped me normalize mental illness and therapy. She's leading a movement through her mental illness as she educates those who may need help and allow them to feel comfortable seeking it." - **Shyann (cousin)**

Chapter SIX

Let's Take It Back: Blacks & The Church

Before I dive into my experience with the church as it relates to my mental health, I think it's important for you to understand the relationship the black community has with the church. It will further explain the responses and reactions I received after disclosing my diagnosis to the community that has been, and still remains, one of the biggest supports.

The black church has been the cornerstone of black history since my ancestors arrived on boats from Africa. According to The Professional Counselor's article entitled "The Black Church: Theology and Implications for Counseling African Americans" by Janeé R. Avent and Craig S. Cashwell, church was supposed to be the one place where blacks could somewhat escape the harsh treatment and commune. Yet, slave masters, their families, and slaves worshipped under the same roof where slaves continued to be treated poorly. Slaves also believed this was an opportunity for slave masters to continue to use their power. This led to slaves creating their own churches to escape mistreatment and have a sacred place to worship. This provided a safe place for my ancestors to be themselves as they supported each other searching for some peace and hope in a horrendous predicament. Some looked forward to death to end their pain and suffering. Hence the famous line from Killmonger in the movie *Black Panther*, "Bury me in the ocean, with my ancestors that jumped from the ships, because they knew death was better than bondage."

During the Civil Rights Movement, African Americans formed predominantly African-American congregations of Baptist, Presbyterian, and Episcopal denominations. Blacks rallied and organized marches and sit-ins at churches. Organizations such as the NAACP received support from the church, as well as individuals who were experiencing financial hardships as we were not allowed to receive government assistance and/or other outside resources. Doesn't it make sense that we rely so much on the church for support? For so many years, it is all the support we had from financial assistance, to building a sense of community and being spiritually fed, in addition to mental health care.

Members of the African American community seek counsel from the church instead of from professionals trained in mental health treatment. This can be problematic because church clergy and leaders may not be trained or knowledgeable in the mental health field. It is not too far-fetched to say church was a place of healing and peace through its emotional and financial support. Several researchers found that African Americans tend to seek professional counseling at a much lower rate than other racial and ethnic populations. In many cases, we believe our relationship with God will help us cope with the challenges of life. In fact, a majority of African Americans identify as Christian, and 50% of African Americans attend church services weekly, according to a Pew Research Center study. We believe that participating in rituals such as attending worship services, devotions, fasting, listening to gospel music, participating in ministries, and listening to sermons will help us during difficult seasons of life. It also allows many to conceptualize struggles within the larger struggle between good and evil, or God and the devil. More importantly, it is safe to say that religious and spiritual resources were used as a form of counseling.

Chapter SEVEN

When Prayer Isn't Enough

"You need to pray harder."

"Those are demons in you."

"Your faith isn't strong enough."

These are a portion of the responses received from church members in the African American community to those who battle with a mental illness such as major depressive and bipolar disorders. It seems some church members tend to minimize or attack a person's faith when individuals who struggle emotionally and mentally seek counsel from the church. While many church leaders in my circle had pure hearts and they genuinely wanted to help, my illness and their lack of understanding, forced me to suffer in silence and pull away from the church. A lack of mental health education leads to myths and contributes to the stigma.

Before I go any further, I want to define the word 'saved' as it is the first word in the title of my book. For those of us who are a part of the Christian faith, we know what it means; but, I cannot assume every person who reads this book is a part of the same faith. In the Christian faith, to be saved means to accept Jesus Christ as your personal Lord and Savior. We believe that God sent his son, Jesus, to die on the cross for our sins, and that we are saved from hell. We also believe that when we die in the physical body, our spirit will go to heaven with Jesus. In the Lexham

Theological Wordbook, when the word 'saved' is used, it involves being saved from the enemy (i.e. the devil) and hell; but, also entering a state of health, wholeness, victory, and safety.

In *The Armor of God,* a bible study by Priscilla Shirer, it says that God's salvation is holistic and involves the well-being of the whole person; not just rescuing them, but even reversing negative circumstances. That's why to be saved and depressed in the Christian faith is not usually accepted and/or denied because we live by scriptures such as Proverbs 18:21, "The tongue has the power of life and death, and those who love it will eat its fruit." While I believe that scripture with every fiber of my being, I also understand that by stating I have depression, I am not "giving myself the illness." It does not mean God cannot heal me or that I lack faith in Him. It is simply my reality, just as a person with cancer will inform someone that they have been diagnosed with the disease. The same principle applies, they aren't "giving themselves cancer." Despite the diagnosis, we believe that we are healed by his stripes (Isiah 53:5) and have the power to speak life into our illness. And despite what the doctor's report says, we are living by and believing God's word which says that we are healed.

I walked up to an older lady to introduce myself and give her a flyer for my event (Save

Our Babies: A Heart To Heart About Suicide Among Children of Color) addressing suicide and mental health for black and Latino children. Her response was, "No, thank you. I just pray for everyone." I was not surprised by her response; however, it made me think about how so many of us in the black Christian community (sometimes) use faith as a crutch. No, I am not saying that prayer does not work, because I am a witness that it does. God spared my life from suicide and has performed countless miracles for me.

For some reason, we tend to think prayer will solve all of our problems. I only believe that statement to be half true because the Bible says, "Faith without works is dead," (James 2:14-26). What do you say to the person who is praying, hearing voices, and seeing things that aren't there and is not finding relief? What do you say to the person who has not showered or eaten in three days? Keep praying? We are more accepting of physical illnesses such as cancer and diabetes, but when it comes to the mind, we deny it and simply act as if mental illness does not exist. Would we tell a person with cancer not to go to chemotherapy? Would we tell the person with a broken leg not to go to the hospital for an x-ray and cast? No, we wouldn't. Yet, when facing an illness that isn't physical, and is in the brain, we are only told to pray.

I get extremely frustrated because I lost my 14-year-old cousin to suicide. When I was suicidal, I was told to speak in tongues for 20 minutes a day and my depression would go away. I was also told that taking medication would make me feel worse. I do not know how to speak in tongues so at that point I said, "Please spare me." I immediately pulled away from the church and eventually God because of the lack of education in the church about mental health. No one in my church community suggested I see a therapist or psychiatrist. Why is that? The brain is an organ just like the heart and liver, and it controls everything in our body.

On an episode of my podcast, Fireflies Unite with Kea, a weekly podcast dedicated to bringing light into darkness (just like actual fireflies) by sharing stories of individuals thriving with mental illness, I interviewed a young lady who mentioned that her family referred to her mental illness as demons. I attended a mental health conference and an attendee stated that her friend decided to share her diagnosis with the pastor since she served as a leader. At the following service, the pastor disclosed this information to the church congregation. Her friend was so hurt that she stopped attending church and to this day, suffers in silence.

On another episode, Pastor Alinicia Gibson of Blessed To Be Gifted Ministry asked, "Is the person who does not take their medication for diabetes, resulting in their death, going to hell?" in response to those who believe that individuals who die by suicide are going to hell. It is important to note that if an individual engages in an unfortunate and harmful activity that ends their life as a result of having a mental illness, it is not their fault. Gibson was diagnosed with bipolar disorder, a mood disorder characterized by episodes of mood swings ranging from depressive lows to manic highs. During manic episodes, individuals may feel a decreased need to sleep, feelings/thoughts of grandeur, unusual talkativeness, and engage in risky activities such as going on shopping sprees and taking sexual risks. However, once the manic episode is over, a person enters a depressive state.

Can God heal those with mental illness? Absolutely, I believe that! There have been stories of people being healed from mental illness, some have been shared on my podcast. However, we must be aware that every person with a mental illness will not be cured. It's unfortunate, yet true. There are instances where some may have to manage their mental illness for the rest of their lives. Seeking mental health treatment along with building your faith can be equally beneficial. We can pray and see a therapist at the same time. I now realize that I do not have to pick one over the other. The church is in a great space because its leaders and members have the power to introduce mental health treatment. I suggest we make some additions when we pray to God when it comes to our mental health. Ask God to direct us to the right therapist and if needed, a psychiatrist to prescribe us the correct medication.

I became free the moment I learned to define my relationship with God instead of allowing a church leader to tell me what it should look like. I spend time with God through praise and worship, journaling, reading the Bible, and devotionals. I never thought I would get to this place because I stopped listening to gospel music, going to church, and did not want to have anything to do with God or church people. I started to rebuild my relationship with God by listening to the Blessed & Bossed Up podcast. It's a podcast that combines entrepreneurship and faith. God started to speak to me through the host, Tatum Temia, and I started to rebuild my relationship with Him. I now also understand that humans are flawed and as stated previously, people in my circle had pure hearts, but lacked the education to assist me.

Here are three ways we can help to merge mental health and the Christian faith:

Start A Mental Health Ministry

The ministry should include licensed clinicians who are faith-based. They are professionals who can help Christians experiencing mental health challenges or mental illness in a way that is not triggering, as well as make the person feel comfortable and refer to the bible for additional support.

Host Mental Health Events

Host events that will help educate and dismantle the mental health stigma, while providing a faith-based component to serve those of the Christian faith.

Train Clergy And Those In Leadership In Mental Health First Aid

At the bare minimum, all individuals who are leaders in the church should have a basic knowledge of mental health and become trained in mental health first aid. Each leader should know where to refer a member of the church if he/she needs counseling or is in a crisis.

Most of all, let's practice empathy and compassion for those with mental illness. It is not made up in our heads and sometimes, it requires more than prayer to heal.

I have spoken at church conferences and I often speak about the story of Elijah, a prophet of God. He was a prophet during the time Ahab ruled over Israel. Ahab and his wife Jezebel worshipped a false god. Elijah went to Ahab and told the people to repent or God would cause a famine so the people would not have food or water. Jezebel did not believe in God and had the prophets killed. Elijah proposed a test to build two altars; one to his God (Jehovah) and one to the false god (Jezebel's god). The priests of the false god called upon their god to send down fire, but there was no answer. When Elijah called on his God, the Lord of Israel, fire came down and burnt up the offering. Jezebel heard of this and planned to have Elijah killed. In 1 Kings 19:3-5, Elijah was afraid and ran for his life. When he came to Beersheba in Judah, he left his servant there and went on a day's journey into the wilderness by himself. He came to a bush, sat down under it and prayed that he might die. "I have had enough, Lord," he said. "Take my life; I am no better than my ancestors." Then he laid down under the bush and fell asleep.

Elijah's statement showcases signs of depression. Two of the many symptoms of depression are hopelessness and feeling suicidal.

Elijah isolated himself which is also a sign of depression. I never heard anyone preach about Elijah's story and speak about depression. If more preachers talked about mental health and told stories of those who experienced mental health challenges in the Bible, people in the church would feel comfortable coming forward. Many do not express their struggles for fear of judgment and having their faith attacked. Instead, we are told things like pray harder, fast, and have more faith. It is safe to say in biblical days, they did not have the diagnoses or advancement in science and technology; therefore, mental illnesses were not given names such as major depressive or bipolar disorders; however, depression symptoms and signs were there, just as shown in Elijah.

It is time we do more than pray. After we pray for someone, give them a referral to see a therapist. After we pray for someone, do not judge them and call them crazy. After we pray for someone, do not gossip about their struggles. After we pray for someone, educate yourself on their mental illness. We must dismantle the mental health stigma especially in the church and stop using prayer as a crutch.

So, the next time someone says, "Pray about it," when it comes to mental health, please kindly remind them that we can pray and see a therapist at the same time.

A Shift Is Happening In The Church

There is a gradual shift happening in the church as people are becoming more accepting and educated on mental health. I consider Dr. Anita Phillips, therapist, speaker, and First Lady of Kingdom Life Church as one of the pioneers leading this conversation. Dr. Phillips' Turn The Light On Movement has taught thousands what the Bible says about mental health. Senior Pastor Keith Battle of Zion Church often states that he attends therapy regularly and Pastor Sarah Jakes-Roberts of One Church L.A. also mentioned counseling as a suggestion to treat depression during a sermon.

The National Alliance on Mental Illness (also referred to as NAMI) is the nation's largest grassroots organization dedicated to building better lives for the millions of Americans affected by mental illness with affiliate state and local county chapters. The local chapters partner with churches to lead educational forums and attend church health events.

While there is a lot of progress to be made in the church, I am happy to see church leaders normalizing the mental health conversation because individuals are less likely to feel conflicted about attending therapy because they were taught to believe therapy showed a lack of faith in God.

Chapter EIGHT

Self–Care...You May Want To Hold Off On The Mani's & Pedi's

In a fast-paced society, it is easy to fall into the hustle and bustle of life. On social media, we are constantly seeing popular hashtags like #grinding, #hustle, and #teamnosleep that so many of us wear as a badge of honor. This used to be me until I had my great awakening, also known as being admitted into the psychiatric unit. I am an extremely goal-oriented person. I do not simply talk about my dreams, I go after them, but that does not mean I cannot take breaks to replenish myself.

Scrolling through social media made me feel like I was not doing enough and taking a break meant I was not working hard. I found myself in a hamster wheel where I was not taking time to sit with my thoughts and emotions. I felt like the Energizer bunny, constantly going after my dreams, working to pay bills and debt without stopping to take care of myself. I was like so many people who walk around being busy, opposed to being productive. I did not know what the term self-care meant, especially since so many limit it to manicures, pedicures, and massages. What I found is that self-care is not limited to those things, but it is self-preservation. Self-care is what feeds your mind, body, and spirit. It is setting boundaries, exercising, having a well-balanced diet, journaling, therapy, having healthy relationships, reading books, and sleeping. What good is a manicure, pedicure, or massage if you are depressed, empty, and broken from trauma?

Where did we get this "brilliant" idea that the less you sleep and take breaks, the more successful you will be? I attribute it to American culture, and for blacks, some of it is linked to being oppressed and having to work twice as hard just to get half of what our oppressors have. It is ingrained in us. There was a time when older generations worked themselves to the bone to provide for their families and overcome racism and oppression. In fact, we are still working to overcome those obstacles. Many of them felt like they did not have time for a mental breakdown, or wrote it off as the blues instead of a mental health condition. Previous generations did not have the luxury of therapy, so church was a form of therapy, as we learned in the previous chapter. While I certainly attribute my relationship with God to being healthy mentally, I also attribute it to addressing my trauma, depression and anxiety disorders, learning my triggers, setting boundaries and developing healthy coping strategies in therapy.

One of the many ways to take care of your mental health is to sleep and take breaks. Sleep is needed for us to function at maximum capacity. According to Healthline, a lack of sleep contributes to memory issues, weight gain, a weakened immune system, increased risk for diabetes, high blood pressure, and so many other health problems. Yet, we wonder why depression, obesity, diabetes, and high blood pressure rates are so high in our community. Being diagnosed with these illnesses is not limited to the foods we eat. We do not make the time to take care of our mental health such as sleep and addressing generational trauma in therapy. I now realize that #grinding, #hustle, and #teamnosleep is ridiculous and is truly killing us. It glorifies being a workaholic and the idea that taking breaks limits your success. I've learned to take breaks and say "no" to replenish my cup. Psalm 23:5 says, "My cup runneth over." I like to say, "What's in my cup is for me and what runs over is for everyone else." Shout-out to Iyanla Vanzant for teaching us this.

In 2018, I accomplished more than I could have imagined, such as meeting Issa Rae and Jenifer Lewis (and interviewed her on my podcast) at the NAACP Image Awards, had over 20 speaking engagements, launched the Fireflies Unite podcast and was featured on Good Morning Washington twice. On a smaller scale, I read over 13 books last year. While reading books may not seem like an accomplishment to many, it has forced me to pull away from social media, spend time with myself, acquire new information, slow down, process my emotions and sit in silence. Most importantly, I have been rebuilding my relationship with God. In the past, I never took the time to pull away from the distractions and noise of life. Managing my mental illness is not easy and I have to make a conscious decision to practice self-care to ensure I am not pouring from an empty cup. However, I no longer deny myself sleep and rest in the name of success.

What will you do to better manage your mental health and ensure you are getting adequate rest?

Chapter NINE

Obesity & Its Impact On Mental Health

"Jenny Craig? You don't need that Kea." At seven-years-old, I told my mother that I needed Jenny Craig to get rid of my fat as we walked past the weight loss and supplements section in Kmart. My mother did her best to reassure me that I was beautiful just the way I was and there was nothing wrong with my weight. I believed her partially because I never thought I was ugly. Do you see my skin? It's flawless! But, I believed I was fat.

By the time I was in fourth grade, I was 100 pounds and around 4 feet tall compared to most of my peers who weighed between 50 and 60 pounds. I will never forget when my classmates and I lined up outside of the nurse's office for our physical examinations. While everyone walked out of the office they shared their weights, I continued to internalize the number on the scale because I weighed the most. When I was 12-years-old, my friend and I went to visit her dad in upstate New York. We were excited to get in the jacuzzi. I grew up in the hood and didn't know anyone with a jacuzzi in their home, so excited is an understatement.

As we were taking off our clothes to get inside the jacuzzi, an overwhelming amount of anxiety came over me as I looked at my bulging stomach and lower gut. My friend and her sister's stomachs were flat. To add fuel to the fire, my friend's sister said, "It's usually more room in the jacuzzi when it's just us two." But here's what I heard, "You're fat and taking up extra room."

In eighth grade, a boy told someone that he would date me if I lost some weight. During that time, I did not think it impacted me; but, I'm sure it did. When my ex-boyfriend and I started having sex, I never wanted the light on and asked him not to touch my stomach. While we did not have the best relationship, he always told me that I was perfect even during moments when we were not intimate.

Since the age of eight, I participated in pageants that did not have swimwear or revealing formal wear. For the formal wear, we wore gowns with crinolines underneath to make it puffy. Yes, I felt like a princess. I did not seek out pageants like this, but I believe it was God's way of surrounding me with people to build my confidence. The pageant staff wanted the participants to be judged on their public speaking skills, talent, and poise instead of their body types. Looking back, I know the pageants helped me to develop discipline, public speaking skills, and confidence. I won three titles and even represented the state of New Jersey. *Flips hair.* I participated in one pageant three times until I won. Talk about dedication. My work ethic is something I am proud of and I attribute my drive to my pageant days. Here's the thing, I know the pageants helped because I became confident in my talents and abilities despite my body image struggles (specifically, my stomach area). Thank you to Ms. V., Ms. Warren, and Ms. Lydia for believing in me, encouraging me to believe in myself, and your endless love and support. I attribute much of my success to them. As I became older, I wasn't sure how I could be so confident in my talents, knowing without a doubt that I was pretty on the outside and inside, but could not get accept my stomach.

In high school, I became extremely active in the dance program at school and my local dance theatre, walked more, and worked out at 5 a.m. with a trainer before school. I lost a ton of weight. I lost so much weight that my head looked huge, like a bobble head. Yes, you can laugh. I felt better about my body, but still I had a hard time with accepting the fat on my stomach. I did my best to mask it with my clothes. Oh yes, I mastered how to put my jeans in a specific area on my stomach so I wouldn't have a fat pouch in the zipper area.

I took showers in the dark because it was relaxing and I enjoyed lying in the tub while the warm water touched my skin. Through therapy, I also realized that I showered in the dark, so I did not have to look at my body when I walked past the mirror. I did not like my rolls. When I looked in the mirror at my stomach and back fat, I saw an overstuffed pack of sausages. Go ahead and laugh again. It's ok. My therapist challenged me to look in the mirror and honor my body by touching it and speaking positive affirmations over it. One of the most powerful statements I said as I touched my stomach was, "I thank you and honor you for getting me this far even though I have not done the best job of taking care of you." In that moment, I realized my body brought me to that point, but if I did not take care of it, I would have major health issues and increase my chances of dying prematurely from a health condition due to being overweight or obese. The doctor told me I was at risk for developing heart disease, diabetes, and other issues if did not get to a healthy weight.

In college, I gained the weight I lost in high school back, plus more. I continued to try diets such as the green smoothie challenge, take garcinia cambogia weight loss pills, B-12 shots, starvation diets, the military diet, and other fad diets that I cannot remember. It got to the point where my weight was like a yo-yo and I felt extreme hopelessness in this area. I lost weight in 2014 as a result of changing my diet and working out because I started to realize that fad diets are not sustainable. By the time I received my diagnoses and was hospitalized for my suicide attempt, I had gained a lot of weight without realizing it. When in a period of depression, I would go days without eating, then binge eat. It became an unhealthy cycle. I thought I would lose weight since I was not eating, little did I know my body would not respond that way. According to Livestrong, you may lose weight initially, but your body responds to starvation by slowing down its metabolism. The body thinks you are entering a state of famine, where food is unavailable. It slows your body's processes to conserve what energy it has stored — in other words, it holds onto fat which results in weight gain.

Finally at 27, I made the decision that I have been considering for three years, to have sleeve gastrectomy which is a weight loss procedure where approximately 75 percent of the stomach is surgically removed along the greater curvature. The result is a sleeve or tube like structure. So in January of 2017, I went to the doctor because I was fed up with my weight and was at my heaviest weight of 240. My knees and lower back hurt because I am short, and it was too much weight for my short frame. I was not happy with myself. I would get out of breath just from walking and was uncomfortable in my body. I never wanted a Teyonna Taylor, Beyoncé, or Instagram model body, but I really desired to be healthy. I feared that I would wake up one morning and be 300 pounds.

For seven months, I met with a dietitian and took nutrition classes, completed a sleep study, abdominal ultrasound, chest x-ray, upper GI, endoscopy, cardiac evaluation and blood work to make sure there were not any internal issues contributing to my weight gain, and I was healthy enough to undergo a major surgery. The nutrition classes helped because I had learned how to read labels and eat foods that will give my body the nutrients it needs. I learned about the things I could not eat such as no raw vegetables for three months after surgery. I learned that exercise did not have to be this intense thing and should not feel like a chore, but would require effort on my part because I had to change my mindset. Did I mention I had to get clearance from my therapist to make sure I was mentally stable for the surgery? I even had to write a letter to my insurance company and doctor explaining why I should be approved for the procedure. Talk about pleading your case...

During my testing process, I discovered that I had nonalcoholic fatty liver disease[14] where

---

[14] Mayo Clinic Fatty Liver Disease
https://www.mayoclinic.org/diseases-conditions/nonalcoholic-fatty-liver-disease/symptoms-causes/syc-20354567

too much fat was stored in my liver cells and I was at risk for health conditions such as high cholesterol, type 2 diabetes, thyroid issues, and sleep apnea. I was diagnosed with asthma at six-years-old, so the extra weight caused more respiratory challenges. I also learned that about 20 percent of people with nonalcoholic fatty liver disease will progress to cirrhosis and even liver cancer. When I say that scared the crap out of me, I was terrified to my core. So the surgery for me was just a tool to assist me with losing weight and reversing some of the damage done to my liver. I am highly aware there is no quick fix to losing weight; however, I knew that if I wanted to see a change, I would have to do something different. Clearly what I was doing in the past wasn't working and I needed to get my emotional eating under control.

Why do you think so many people go for the cakes and cookies when they are feeling sad or depressed? Because many of us are looking to fill an emotional void. And when that void isn't filled, we overeat and stuff ourselves until we are overweight, obese, living with diabetes, hypertension, and/or heart disease. So our diet has more to do with our mental health than we may think. Ask yourself, *am I eating my pain?* When you are feeling anxious, lonely and/or depressed what foods do you grab? Have you ever eaten to the point where you couldn't breathe? I would overeat and start wheezing and immediately, I needed my asthma inhaler.

My doctor told me that after the procedure I could not eat bread, pasta, or rice for one year. You read right. ONE YEAR! Did I mention no fried foods either? Breads, pasta, and rice do not have a lot of nutritional value and would expand in my new tiny stomach. She also said that I could not have alcohol for one year which wasn't an issue because I was on psychotropic medications and stopped drinking after my suicide attempt. The list continued to grow. I could not get pregnant for 18 months after the procedure as my body would go through a major change. I didn't think I wanted kids so I said, "We're good on that, doc." I also went on a liquid diet for four weeks to shrink my liver.

The doctor explained that there are instances when they cannot get to the stomach because the liver is enlarged as a result of nonalcoholic fatty liver disease. So in some cases, they have to abort the surgery and reschedule it. I did not that want to happen to me. I was determined despite how challenging it would be because at that point, I needed a healthy liver.

That liquid diet was the hardest thing I ever did because I felt the urge to chew something.

Have you tried only eating sugar free popsicles and jello and drinking protein smoothies, diluted apple juice and Gatorade for four weeks? To me, this was not the easy way out. I was willing to make the commitment to change for my health. If you are considering a weight loss procedure, ask yourself, once I lose the weight, will I go back to eating things like greasy foods, snacking on cookies every night, over consuming starches and juices?

I lost 12 pounds before the surgery. The surgery was a success. I was sore for a month and became easily dehydrated, which put me in the hospital (like many bariatric patients) because I had a hard time consuming liquids. Since my stomach was smaller, I could not eat a lot. Knowing portion control was an issue for me, I did not mind having a boost of help in this area. The second phase was pureed foods which meant I could eat things like mashed potatoes with a scoop of protein powder, tuna and beans. I was pretty much eating like a baby at that point, reintroducing my body to foods. I also decided that I would no longer eat meat anymore and gradually removed dairy from my diet. Today, my nutritionist continues to help me as I make changes to be completely plant-based. I stopped eating meat nine months prior to my surgery, but I gained weight because I ate too many starchy foods. And since the procedure restricted me from eating bread, pasta and rice, I knew this was the perfect opportunity to change my diet.

Three months after surgery, I ran into complications that caused me to go into the hospital. With a new stomach, my body rejected some foods and one night, I woke up screaming from excruciating stomach pain. I could not breathe, I was sweating, pacing back and forth in my room and crying. I called 9-1-1 and was rushed to the hospital only to be told that I was constipated. I know, you're probably laughing and saying, "Kea, this is too much information." This is also common for bariatric patients. It happened again two more times and I was not constipated. After running multiple tests, they said everything looked good. Yet morphine was the only medicine to knock the pain out. I do not know what giving birth feels like, but I was screaming like a baby was coming out.

After speaking with my doctors, we concluded that it was most likely from me eating too fast. I'd been instructed at least 15 times between my doctor's appointments and nutrition classes to take 30 minutes to eat each meal and chew 30 times before swallowing. It may not make sense to someone who hasn't experienced being overweight or obese. Slowing down when eating causes your brain to communicate with your stomach that it is full and prevents you from overeating. It also prevents foods from having a hard time going down the sleeve which was extremely painful. This was challenging for me because I have always finished my food in less than five minutes. I eat every meal as if it is going to be my last. This procedure and the challenges after the surgery forced me to be a mindful eater. This experience has been trial and error and even with the few complications, I would not trade it for the world. It has been a great tool for me.

I joined a Facebook group to talk to women who had gastric sleeve or bypass. I informed my mom and a handful of people of my decision. I have a friend who went through the process and she supported me. I also joined a support group at the hospital where I had the procedure. I've heard horror stories of people who died during the procedure or people who gained all of their weight back. I battled with a lot of shame at first because I knew some people would say I was taking the easy way out. In therapy, I learned not to care what others thought about my journey as I was doing this for my health, not to be a supermodel. Of course, I want to look good. Who doesn't? I also wanted to feel good and feel changes internally. Why is it that we praise people for getting boob and butt jobs, but look down on people who have weight loss surgery?

I asked myself, *Why should I worry about what people think about me?* In the words of the powerful Lisa Nichols, "It is none of my business what others think of me." It was time for me to let go of my fears and anxieties and care less what people thought about me. I decided not to keep it a secret anymore and shared it publicly on social media because I was no longer ashamed. In the beginning, I intentionally did not tell anyone who would discourage me, feed my insecurities or judge me. It was very similar to keeping my mental illness a secret and it almost killed me. My weight gain was definitely a gradual suicide. I did not want to increase my chances of diseases that come from being obese such as certain cancers and diabetes. Though I may not blast that I had weight loss surgery all over social media constantly or wear it on a t-shirt, I am proud of myself for making this change to become a better me.

I wouldn't say that my depression and anxiety was linked to me being obese, but it impacted how I viewed myself. I hid behind black, loose fitting clothes. I was becoming a different person because I love wearing bright colors. I refused to buy anymore jeans when I reached a size 18. I wore leggings every day to keep from facing the fact that my jean size increased and it was hard for me to breathe when wearing jeans. I was obese. Yes, I was. Not 600 pounds obese but weighing 240 pounds at 5'2" was big enough to scare me and make me fed up.

Six weeks after the surgery, my doctor gave me clearance to exercise and I have been working out consistently ever since. I've set the goal of working out four times per week and joined a gym with boot camp classes. I wake up at 4:45 a.m. Monday through Thursday to attend my class at 5:15 a.m. and I love it! I found a gym with people who hold me accountable and encourage me. I knew that if exercise felt like a chore, I wasn't going to do it. The option of classes seemed like the way to go. Just like I need air and water to survive, I knew that I needed to make exercise a part of my routine. Exercise has additional benefits besides losing weight such as better sleep, focus, better management of sugar and blood levels, and improved mood.

Improving my mood is important to me because exercise releases "feel good" chemicals (e.g. serotonin and endorphins) that make us feel happy. When depression comes along with its ugly face, it decreases the amount of serotonin I produce so the medication increases it. The natural chemicals my body releases from working out are perfect for my depression and anxiety. No, exercise is not a cure for major depressive disorder, but it certainly helps. And since I plan to work my way off medication (with the help of my doctor), then working out is a necessity. I am proud of the 50 pounds I've lost in six months. I manage my stress better and am happy with the woman I see in the mirror. It's not all about the weight. It is also about the inches and non-scale victories. Non-scale victories are milestones that show I am losing weight and inches. Things like, I have one roll on my back instead of three. It's okay to laugh. I laugh every time I tell people this. My back and knee pains stopped completely and I can fit into jeans that I have not been able to wear in four years. I can walk up more than five steps without feeling like I ran a marathon since my endurance has increased.

I also knew a plant-based diet would help me in continuing to lose and sustain a healthy weight. I am approximately 75 to 80 percent plant-based as I still consume seafood and have limited my dairy intake between two to three times per month. I removed cow's milk completely from my diet, replacing it with almond milk. I added meat substitutes and Pinterest has become my best friend as I try new vegan and vegetarian recipes. I want to eliminate as much of the added hormones, preservatives, and sugars used in meat and dairy. I even changed the make-up, toiletries, feminine, and cleaning products I use to decrease my chances of being diagnosed with certain cancers that are associated with the chemicals used in those products. As a result, I see huge differences in my health such as losing weight, clear skin, less bloating and brain fog. It's not easy, but I am happy with the transition. With research and time, I am planning to work my way to being 100% plant-based as I am on a journey to heal my mind, body, and spirit holistically.

Did you know...

- ➤ depression and low self-esteem have been observed in obese patients, even when there has been no previous history of mental illness?[15]
- ➤ patients with a history of attention-deficit/hyperactivity disorder (ADHD) have a greater chance of becoming obese?[16]
- ➤ in women, obesity can lead to problems in the reproductive system?[17]
- ➤ severe cases of obesity can reduce your life expectancy, particularly if you are a young adult?[18]
- ➤ binge eating, a behavior associated with both obesity and other conditions such as

---

[15]American Psychological Association:
https://www.apa.org/helpcenter/obesity.aspx
[16] Ibid
[17] Ibid
[18]Ibid

anorexia nervosa, is also a symptom of depression?[19]

➢ 51% of people who are obese with binge eating problems also had a history of major depression?[20]

➢ research shows that obese women with binge-eating disorder who experienced teasing about their appearance later developed body dissatisfaction and depression?[21]

Could I have lost the weight without the procedure? My answer is no because as I have stated before, I'd lost weight and gained it back plus more. I've never lost this much weight or remained consistent with a well-balanced diet and workout schedule for this long. I am going on eight months of this new lifestyle and it has positively impacted my mental health so much. I am incredibly productive and have greater mental clarity.

Notice that I did not say deprivation. Before, when I deprived myself of things, it only made my internal fight harder and I ended up binge eating what I took away. Having had the surgery restricts me from some things, but this is what I needed to restart my life. Honestly, I'm

---

[19] Ibid
[20] Ibid
[21] Ibid

afraid of not following instructions just to end up doing damage to myself. Who wants to undergo a major surgery, then cause more damage to themselves? Not me. The surgery has helped people become healthy by reducing diabetes, curing sleep apnea, high cholesterol, and of course, weight loss.

On the other hand, there have been people who had the procedure, lost weight, and gained it back. Let me be clear, if I go back to my old eating habits, the weight will come back. The surgery itself is not a cure.

Someone in the Facebook bariatric group wrote, "What advice should I give my friend who had gastric bypass and wants to undergo another surgery because she gained all of her weight back?" My advice was, "I encourage you to suggest therapy to your friend so she can get to the root of her relationship with food."

Let me be the first to tell you if no one has, weight loss will not take away your insecurities or make you happier. Yes, I've lost weight, but guess what? I still have a gut. Yes, a gut. Remember my stomach story I told you about earlier in this chapter? While it has gotten slightly smaller, it is still there. I learned to embrace my stomach no matter where I am in my journey. I look in the mirror with the light on and honor my body. I rub s h e a b u t t e r coconut oil on my stomach and tell myself you are beautiful and I love every roll and imperfection. I honor my temple (mind, body, and spirit) that God has given me by attending therapy to address issues, eating the right foods and working out consistently. It has provided me with a holistic approach so that all areas of my life are addressed. I thank God for this tool and it is my prayer that I will continue to take care of myself.

Chapter TEN

Therapy (And Medication) Saved My Life

Therapy is for crazy and rich white people. I'm neither of those things, so I must not need therapy, right? My first introduction to therapy was in elementary school. My mother raised my cousin. I remember she began taking my cousin to an office to create arts and crafts as I sat in the waiting area. I wanted to go into the office to participate; but, I could not and often wondered why. At the time, I did not realize it was therapy because no one told me and I never asked. I wonder if I received therapy as a child how different my life would be. However, I believe God doesn't make mistakes. I know this to be true because Romans 8:28 tells me, "And we know that for those who love God all things work together for good, for those who are called according to his purpose."

I wasn't completely against therapy; I was fearful of letting people know that I was going to therapy. Anytime someone asked where I was going, I would only respond, "To the doctor." The word 'therapy' never came out of my mouth. I was always surprised when I overheard people say they were in therapy. Actually, I only heard it from white people. I went to my first therapy session at the counseling center on Howard University's campus during my junior year because I experienced a lot of deaths in a short time period. I needed someone to talk to about my thoughts and emotions. I didn't talk about feeling depressed or suicidal because I was fearful of being forced into the hospital, so I limited what I shared. I also joined a grief group and it helped to be around others who I could relate to.

After I graduated from Howard, I tried a few therapists and didn't make any progress. I attribute it to not being in a space to heal, being undiagnosed, and unable to connect with the therapists. I worked with a white man and woman, and found that I often felt worse after leaving my sessions with the man. In sessions with the woman, I only talked about surface level things because I was uncomfortable. Overall, I did not make any progress with either one of them.

Prior to my hospitalization, I found a therapist who I felt comfortable sharing everything with. Shout out to Dr. Tucker! I preferred to work with a black woman. In fact, I prefer a black woman for my overall care from my primary doctor and gynecologist. Finding a therapist is almost like dating and can be discouraging for some. I'm not stating that people of color can't make progress with clinicians who are white, it's just imperative that they are culturally aware.

According to the Substance Abuse and Mental Health Services Administration, cultural awareness is the ability to interact effectively with people of different cultures and helps to ensure that the needs of all community members are addressed. Cultural awareness means to be respectful and responsive to the health beliefs and practices—and cultural and linguistic needs—of diverse populations. This will help to ensure damage isn't done to the client due to the clinician's lack of knowledge about the client's culture. For example, during a podcast interview, I spoke with a psychiatrist who mentioned that her colleague believed his client lost the concept of time because the client stated that he hadn't smoked weed "in a minute." The psychiatrist explained to her colleague that when black people say they haven't done something in a minute, it does not mean an actual minute. A minute could mean a few months. This is just one small example, but what would have happened if she wasn't there? Think about how many situations like this happen. These are instances where clients can easily be misdiagnosed.

Honestly, I did not start seeing changes with therapy until after I was prescribed the correct medication by the psychiatrist at the hospital and I took it as prescribed. I was given medication for my depression, anxiety, and to help me sleep. I stopped taking the medication for sleep a year after because I found a sleep routine that helped me and I wanted to limit the amount of medication that I was taking. I was against medication initially because I felt ashamed for needing it to make me feel "normal" enough to function. I asked myself, *What's wrong with you?* And, *why can't you be strong like everyone else?* I felt weak because I needed pills to do simple things like shower and brush my teeth.

Eventually, I accepted my truth and told myself that it was okay. People take pills for headaches and other health conditions---this was no different. While I have the goal of getting off my medication, I no longer judge myself for needing to take it. During a time when I stopped taking the medication, against my doctor's guidance, I saw a rapid decline. It left me in the bed for four days until a friend came to my home to check on me. I did not shower, eat, or go to work; my suicidal thoughts came back. My body was going through a withdrawal. I was shaking, experienced body chills, and felt like I had the flu. I will never go off my medication without the guidance of my doctor. Because of this experience, I have a new perspective and compassion for those who are sick with addiction and experience withdrawal during detox.

Recently, I spoke with my therapist and told her that I am considering speaking with my psychiatrist to transition off of my medication. She agreed because I am in a better place in my recovery. I am excited and ready; however, if I notice myself declining, there is no shame in getting back on my medication. I used to think medication was only for people who saw things that were not there, heard voices and talked to themselves. Little did I know that medication (referred to as psychotropics) for mental illness is what some people need. Some will be on medication for the rest of their lives and that's okay. Those two pills truly helped to save my life.

After I was discharged from the hospital for my suicide attempt, I also went to therapy weekly and saw my psychiatrist once a month. I experienced moments of being frustrated and thought therapy wasn't working. Because my battle with depression and anxiety began in middle school, I knew getting to a happier place wasn't going to happen overnight. What I've learned through therapy is talking about your challenges and trauma is only one part of the healing process. By talking about my issues, I realized patterns in my behaviors, irrational thinking, the necessity to create boundaries, develop healthy coping strategies, and identify my triggers.

One of my biggest triggers was my siblings' dad, not to be confused with my stepfather, as that title needs to be earned. I do not call him my stepdad and will correct anyone who does. I made the difficult decision to no longer stay at my mother's house when I visit my family in New Jersey. I enjoy being around my brothers and sister, but the toxic environment contributed to my anxiety. My mother was hurt, but she understood that I had to what was best for me. Even though my siblings' dad did not do anything to me directly, he caused me a lot of emotional pain because of the way he treated my mom and siblings.

When it came to boundaries, I started telling people "no" which was an area I struggled with before. I used to say "yes" to everything, even if I was tired or sick. Through therapy, though, I learned to put myself first. I put this into practice by saying no, I was not going to stay at my mother's house. If I say no, it is not because I am being mean and don't want to help someone. It means I do not have the emotional or mental bandwidth to do what is being asked of me.

I now understand boundaries are guidelines for my safety and well-being. For instance, since I work out Monday through Thursday at 5 a.m., on Sunday through Wednesday, my phone automatically goes on 'Do Not Disturb' at 9:00 p.m. so I can wake up at 4:45 a.m. This helps to ensure I get the same amount of sleep each night and do not wake up groggy. Simply put, boundaries are self-care as they set the tone for how you treat yourself and allow others to treat you.

Therapy does not work unless you put in the work. My therapist challenged my thinking and helped me to see things differently. She informed me of areas that I needed to work on such as becoming self-aware, having a better relationship with myself, friends, and even letting go of people who no longer serve me. Therapy also provided me with a safe space where I did not have to worry about being judged or hear things like, "I wouldn't do that if I was you," or "What's wrong with you?" and, "You have nothing to be depressed about." Overall, I can say when I look at the mirror, I am proud of the woman I see because I am beautiful from the inside out. I am operating from a place of wholeness instead of brokenness, so the decisions I make are from a healthier mental space.

Chapter ELEVEN

Finding Peace In My Singleness & Celibacy

I was scrolling through Twitter and saw two articles from xonecole.com. The first headline read, "All My Single Ladies: Real Women Reflect On Being Single for 3+ Years" and the other read, "You Can't Sex It Away: A Dick Appointment Is Not An Antidepressant." The first article stood out to me because I am single and have been celibate for almost two years. My eyes almost popped out of my head at the second title. Whew child! Before I go any further, you may be asking how this relates to mental health. Romantic, family, or friend relationships certainly impact our mental health. We all have the desire to feel wanted, needed, valued, and be a part of community that accepts us for who we are, flaws and all. Whether it's an entrepreneurship community, church, or #team (insert whatever your zodiac sign, hometown or college is), fraternity, sorority, gym, or favorite sports team. What are communities comprised of? Relationships, right?

Did you know…

> studies show that people with healthy relationships heal faster, have lower blood pressure, are less likely to experience a depression relapse, and feel less anxious than those who don't?[22]

---

[22] Canopy Health:
https://www.canopyhealth.com/en/members/articles/building
-healthy-relationships-can-increase-your-mental-health.html

> having relationships with people and having a conversation with an empathetic listener can help relieve stress and help you process your emotions by engaging in activities with friends (such as walking or playing sports), increases your energy, and releases tension?[23]

> relationships help provide people with purpose and meaning?[24]

Relationships have more impact on your mental health than you may think. Essentially, everything impacts our mental health and it is my hope that after reading this book you will begin to connect the dots. In instances when we do not feel supported or valued, it tends to feed our feelings of loneliness and sadness, which contribute to depression. How could it be that you are surrounded by people who love you but still feel lonely? This happens when needs are not being met.

In terms of romantic relationships, sometimes, when we are single for extended periods, we began to internalize our singleness and think something is wrong with us. We may ask things like, "What's wrong with me? Why can't

---

[23] Ibid
[24] Ibid

I get a man?" As we scroll through social media and see our friends getting engaged, married and/or starting families, some of us may not realize that we are idolizing a wedding day without grasping all the actual work that goes into a marriage. I have to navigate relationships differently because of my struggles with mental illness such as when to disclose my illness and my struggles with suicidal thoughts. One of the women in the article stated that she's been single for four years; like real single, no boo thing, no bae, nothing. She experienced toxic relationships in the past, so she took a break to heal and work on herself. She said that when she decided to take a break, she had no idea it would be for four years. She said during the break she worked on her finances, her weight, and worked on herself in general to have peace of mind. She also said she's at a point in her life where she desires a romantic relationship, but for whatever reason it's not happening for her. In her world of wedding planning, love is constantly in her face. She said she loves seeing people in love, yet can't help but wonder when it will be her turn.

I could relate as this topic was something I struggled with. As I've stated before, we are so focused on the wedding itself, because of what we see on social media, that it's easy to negate the work and the sacrifices in a long term relationship or marriage. The divorce rate in this country is 40 to 50 percent. Since, that's nearly half of the people who get married, I want to make sure that I am mentally and emotionally stable when I am dating someone who I may end up marrying. When I get married, I plan to be in that relationship until death do us part.

In my early twenties, I was so desperate to be in a relationship because I was a late bloomer. Relationships were not my focus in high school or college; I was focused on school and career. By the time I was 23, I felt like I was playing catch up and got into a relationship with a lovely fellow I met on okcupid.com. Let's call him, Mr. Soccer Player. That's all he talked about and played. He was from a country in Africa. Don't ask me which country because I don't remember. Anyway, I wanted what I saw on social media: the happy couple and perfect family. I found myself in a relationship with somebody who I really didn't take the time to get to know. I was battling loneliness, depression, and anxiety, but I was not diagnosed at this time. I compromised my values because I feared losing a man I thought I loved. A man who broke up with me two days after I gave my virginity to him. Honestly, I still don't completely know why he broke up with me. He claimed he wasn't ready for a relationship.

I can laugh at it now, but if this would have happened in high school or in college, I would not have been able to handle it. Of course, I was disappointed when it happened, but I did not feel like my life was over. I think this was because we did not have a lot of history. We were only dating for a few months. What I learned from that experience with my ex is not to allow anyone or a staged picture on social media to rush me into a relationship with anybody just for the sake of saying I have a boo. Yes, I battle with depression and anxiety, and I don't know if it will ever go away because I've been battling it since childhood. It's not all of me, but it's certainly a part of who I am. The person who I date and eventually end up marrying will have to accept this part of me and we will have to figure out how to handle those challenges when they arise.

After my ex broke up with me, I received my diagnosis a few months later. And guess what? We were still sleeping together. I did not want to be in a relationship; but, I enjoyed having him around because it was a great distraction. It was a waste of time because the sex was terrible and it prolonged my healing process. Anytime I wanted an escape or felt lonely, I sent a text and he knew what that meant. It was the kind of relationship we established for about two years. Sometimes we'd go without talking for six months or more. Then, at some point, I had to stop using him and deal with my problems.

Recently, he sent me a text message that said, "Hey, what's up?" We haven't talked in over a year so I asked myself, *Kea, do you really want to engage with this?* First, I don't love him. In fact, I never did. Second, if I text him, I will end up having sex with him. And third, I don't enjoy sex with him. I've worked so hard on myself and now I desire a commitment. Replying to his text message would have been a waste of time and energy, so I ignored the text. The broken Kea would have responded, then got mad at myself. I have nothing against my ex and wholeheartedly wish him the best. I know entertaining him would not serve me or push me closer to anything God has for me.

In 2017, I was dating a guy who I was falling in love with. Let's call him, Mr. Sexy Chocolate because obviously, he was sexy and chocolate. Just writing about him, gives me chills. Anyway, I enjoyed his company, he made me laugh, was driven, successful, and did I mention fine? And to be honest, the sex was great. But he treated me like a convenience store. Twice he went ghost for months, popping back in when he felt like it, saying he left because I was pressuring him for a relationship. And guess what? I allowed it.

I expressed the desire to be in a committed relationship; he claimed he didn't have time working full-time and being in graduate school full-time. When we were together, things were perfect and I felt like I was on a cloud; but, I allowed him to control my emotions and it became unhealthy. I would feel so high, then feel so low because he was emotionally unavailable. This was during a time I decided that I did not need my medication, so you know what happened, right? This led to an increase of suicidal thoughts, lack of motivation, inability to do simple tasks such as shower and cook. I decided to open up to him about my mental health challenges with hopes of receiving compassion and support. It did not change anything, and eventually I decided to let him know that I was no longer accepting being treated like a convenience store. I put him on my block list and it hurt.

In the end, he wanted a friend with benefits, only he never stated it. I thought Mr. Sexy Chocolate was my future husband and I still have moments of thinking about him wishing it had worked out. At some point, I had to put myself first, focus on my healing and learn to set the standard of how I will be treated. A man will only do what I allow, so I take full responsibility for allowing someone to treat me less than.

I decided to be celibate to protect myself after I blocked Mr. Sexy Chocolate. This would help me determine who was dating me to get to know me versus dating me for sex. As I started to redevelop my relationship with God, I decided to remain celibate for God so I could grow spiritually and focus on myself. I also knew being celibate was best for me because sex can be a distraction. With both men I dated, sex clouded my judgement. Since I was depressed when dealing with them, I did not make the best decisions. I was not happy with myself, so I thought getting into a relationship with someone would cure my depression. It did not. Happiness was beneath the trauma, hurt, insecurities and mask that I wore daily. Until I went beneath the surface to address what I've suppressed, I would have continued to look for happiness in another man, degree, house, pair of shoes, or job title.

I was talking to my friend and she explained how she always felt the need to be in a relationship and couldn't spend an extended amount of time being single. It made me think about how so many women who feel that way settle for the sake of having a man. They are afraid to be alone with the woman in the mirror. Some even find that they are constantly in a cycle of unhealthy relationships. How is that I am single, have been celibate for almost two years and I am the happiest that I've ever been in my entire life? Is it easy? Absolutely not, but I've done too much work on myself, know my value, and refuse to allow someone to disrupt the peace that I work so hard to create in my life. I desire a healthy relationship with a man who honors God, respects and supports me, and pushes me to grow in God, personally and professionally. I will do the same for him.

When we are operating from a place of brokenness instead of wholeness, we often make terrible decisions in relationships. We make decisions based on fear or comparing our relationship to those on our timelines. For example, I've mentioned on a few podcast episodes and to family and friends that I don't have the desire to have children. You may be shocked reading this too. Here's the thing, I am willing to make a compromise with my significant other, to have one child, but who knows? As the oldest of seven children and godmother of two, I highly doubt it. I have been changing diapers since I was nine-years-old. I love my role as a big sister and godmother who has the ability to influence and shape the lives of the little ones around me. The beauty in all of this is that I can change my mind; I'm only 28-years- old.

Overtime, I realized that I allowed society and what I saw in the media to define what a woman should be. I thought if I didn't want children, I would be less of a woman. Growing up, I often talked about having children because I thought it was something I needed to do. The older I've become, the more the desire seems to dissipate. There's nothing wrong with that and it does not mean that I'm less of a woman because I don't want to have children. My value and womanhood is not defined by whether I have children or not, neither will my marriage be. I don't see myself being a soccer mom the way some women do and that's okay. Again, it's really important that we define motherhood, our careers and success for ourselves without seeking validation from others.

While I have the desire to be married, I also value my singleness because it's the perfect time to focus on myself. It may sound cliché, but being single allows me to work on being the best version of myself in preparation for my future husband. I am now genuinely happy and no longer seek a relationship to escape my problems.

During this time, I'm focusing on rebuilding my credit because for almost two years I was out of work and lived paycheck to paycheck. That meant I couldn't pay my bills on time. I had to rob

Peter to pay Paul. Now that I'm no longer living paycheck to paycheck, I have the ability to do simple things like put my bills on autopay. That is definitely #goals for me. I couldn't do that before because I was pinching pennies. I'm working with a financial coach who is holding me accountable for my budget, saving an emergency fund, and building a plan to save and purchase my first home in four years. I have decreased my debt and look forward to knocking more debt off the list. I'm also planning my first trip outside the country this year to the Dominican Republic! I've been to Puerto Rico, but it's a U.S. territory, so I don't count it as out of the country even though it is.

More importantly, during this time, I'm rebuilding my relationship with God. To do this, I am spending time reading His word, learning how to pray strategically and recently have been able to recognize His voice again. I'm not saying that you can't focus on these things when you are in a relationship, but it is easier to focus on yourself since relationships require time, energy, and sacrifice. And while I have the time to focus on myself, why not focus on my goals instead of being one of two broken people who enter a relationship? Then, not only would I have to work on the relationship, I'd have to work on myself too. If you add children to the picture, it makes things more complex along with the risk of raising broken children. That is a recipe for disaster. For those who are married, it could lead to a divorce.

Focusing on my mental, emotional, spiritual, and physical health now means that is less work I will have to do when I get into a relationship. Many times, we get into relationships and think, *If I just had a boo thing, everything would be okay.* But it would not. It would only bring your insecurities to the forefront.

I have a few questions for you: Are you dealing with anxiety? Do you feel defeated? Do you feel depressed? Are you coming out of a divorce and need to grieve? What thoughts come to your mind anytime you feel lonely or not good enough for a relationship? Can you be happy for other couples or find that you are jealous?

I want to encourage you to journal because it will help you to identify patterns in your thinking and behaviors. Also, ask yourself what goals you want to accomplish, personally and professionally. Then list out what small steps you can take to accomplish those goals. Maybe it's starting a YouTube channel, going to therapy consistently, traveling more, or building your savings account.

Chapter TWELVE

Trust The Process: It's Working For Your Good

In college, when people asked me what I wanted to do after graduation, I told them my goal was to be the head of production or communications at a television network and own a production company. I had dreams of moving to California and working my way up the corporate ladder to be the HBIC (head beauty in charge). You could not tell me that I was not going to be Miranda Priestly from the movie *The Devil Wears Prada*. I was going to be a boss running the office in my pencil skirts, suits, pumps, silk pressed hair bouncing with every step, and all the confidence in the world. I thought after graduation, life was going to be popping! But as I'm sure you know, life tends not to pan out exactly as you envision.

I moved to California after graduation to work for a public access television station with the hopes that my career would eventually take off after my year of service with AmeriCorps, a year-long community service project. When I arrived to California, I learned a huge lesson. GET EVERYTHING IN WRITING! My former supervisor made promises of helping me find a place to stay until I found an apartment and got a car. However, when I arrived, I had to figure it out on my own. I stayed with two coworkers who I'd recently met, had no car or money, and was hanging on by a thread. I would not have a paycheck until a few weeks later and when I ran out of places to stay, I stayed at a hotel that I discovered was under investigation for prostitution. I left that hotel to stay at a Holiday Day Inn Express.

During this time, I was suicidal. I deactivated all of my social media accounts, wrote a Facebook status that implied I was going to end my life, ignored phone calls except from my mom, and felt hopeless. My Howard University sister, Breann, texted me the National Suicide Prevention Lifeline and it was the first time I called. It did not help me at all. I felt worse during and after the call. I will say this: that was my experience with one person. There are countless volunteers on the lifeline who can help, and I would try it again if I became suicidal.

At that time, I was not diagnosed. As I stated in the previous chapter, my suicidal thoughts started as a child. Anytime life became overwhelming, my mind immediately went to suicide. I could not control it.

Let's get back to California. I thought I was going to be homeless and have no choice but to stay in a shelter. My pride would not allow me to stay in a shelter. I did not have any family in California, but I knew a few people there from college. I did not want to go back home after being there for only two weeks, so I told myself I would stick it out. After speaking with Breann, her family agreed to let me to stay with them until I found an apartment and purchased a car. Thank you to my Cali mom and dad (Terri and Donald Norwood).

Los Angeles is five and half hours from San Jose, so I took the Greyhound bus. And if you know anything about Greyhound, it makes multiple stops and takes longer routes than being in a car. It took me about nine hours on the bus to travel to L.A. I told my job that I needed to take one month off. Since I needed to attend a training in L.A., it seemed to be the best option.

When I arrived to L.A., a sense of peace came over me because I was with someone who loved me. Shortly after, I found an apartment on craigslist with a young lady who was looking for a roommate and purchased my first car within three weeks. I used the relocation money provided by the AmeriCorp program for the deposit on the apartment and my mother and great-uncle gave me the down payment for my car. I had a video call with my possible new roommate, and it seemed like a fit so I agreed to rent out the other bedroom in her apartment.

When I arrived back to San Jose, I was a little hopeful and thought things had to gradually get better. I was excited to get back to work and put my production degree to use. I was teaching a video production class to fourth graders, and interviewing local and state candidates in California elections. I was also the technical director for the public access television station that captured high school football games and local community events, like parades and festivals. I enjoyed the job, but having a lack of finances added to my stress and increased my suicidal thoughts. I was constantly late on my rent, my car loan, and had a challenging time purchasing groceries. I went to social services and was approved for food stamps. Talk about a blessing! I did not have the desire to live off of them; I needed them until my finances improved.

This wasn't the picture I envisioned for my life. I decided to get a second job to make ends meet. After being told that I could not obtain a second job during my year of service with AmerCorp, my California dream seemed to fade. That Jersey hustler in me kept me going though. I reached out to my contacts and booked freelance gigs to work on the Soul Train Awards in Las Vegas and BET Honors in Washington, D.C. When I arrived back from D.C., my roommate had changed the locks on me. Of course I called the police to assist, but they stated since my name was not on the lease, I could not enter the home. I had no idea where I was going to go for the night. Honestly, I do not know exactly why she changed the locks. I think it was because I asked her if she could lower the rent or if I could leave the apartment earlier than planned.

Thankfully, I had recently joined a church and one of the ladies at the church allowed me to stay with her. I had to get legal representation because my roommate decided to withhold all of my mail. Thank God, I packed all of my items and put them in my car before I left for D.C., so I did not have any valuables in the apartment. After my roommate received the letter from my attorney that holding mail is a federal offense, she returned it to the attorney's office.

Unfortunately, I could no longer manage my stress level and decided to move back home to New Jersey to figure out my next steps. I felt like a failure because it did not work out. I had no idea what I wanted to do, but staying in a toxic house with my siblings' dad was not an option. I booked a location scouting coordinator gig for a production company in New York. If you don't know the way freelance gigs work, you get a job for a specific length of time then move on to your next project. While I enjoyed it, the lack of stability and security pushed me to return to school.

I applied for the Master's of Professional Studies Program in Public Relations and Corporate Communications at Georgetown University. I fell into the trap thinking that if I had another degree, I would be more marketable for a job in my field. On the other hand, my student loan debt doubled before I could make any payments on my student loans from my undergraduate degree. After graduation from graduate school, I did not have an exact plan. I just knew I wanted to own my own company. So that's what I did.

Summoning my childhood dream of being that Miranda Priestly I'd envisioned, I opened a public relations firm. It didn't take long before I learned valuable lessons about being careful who you hire for projects, how to develop a brand and legalize a business, how to build a website, and the importance of including God, not only in my life, but in my business. I ended up closing the firm before it really got off the ground. Once again, I felt like a failure because something else did not work out for me.

Since we live in the social media era, we expect life to work the same way for us as it appears to do for others. We expect instant gratification and are disappointed when life doesn't happen on our scheduled timeline. Through this process, I discovered that I am not a failure, I am simply human. Oprah did not become an Oprah overnight success. In fact, she was fired from her evening news reporter gig with Baltimore's WJZ-TV at 23-years-old because she got too emotionally invested in her stories. A

Baltimore TV producer reportedly told her she was "unfit for television news," according to the book *Become Your #1 Fan*.[25] Steve Jobs was in his 30s when Apple, the company he co-founded, fired him before he returned and launched the iPhone.[26] The point is, despite what you may see on social media and television, unless you were born rich, success will require work. But even if you are rich, it will never fill voids; money will be a cover up for your broken areas.

"Your business cannot grow past the point that you haven't healed," was stated by a guest on the Patrice Washington's Redefining Wealth podcast. This could not be more true. Once I committed to my healing and reconnected with God, the blessings started pouring out. So many of us want the success in our careers, but do not want to or have not done our soul work. Your soul work is beneath the fake smile, hidden in the new car you buy every year, salary increases, and empty relationships you look to find your value in.

My journey has taught me the value of not being afraid to share every part of me because shame and guilt will continue to feed my insecurities and broken areas. By talking about it

[25] Inc:
https://www.inc.com/business-insider/21-successful-people-who-rebounded-after-getting-fired.html
[26] Ibid

gave me the space to heal, walk boldly in my God-given purpose, and inspire others along the way. Who would have thought that I would merge my experience of living with mental illness with my communications and media skills to raise awareness for mental health? What initially started as a podcast and speaking business has transpired into a vision that I never thought would happen: a mental health media and communications company. This is something new that I haven't seen done before, but it fits me so well.

Through my transparency, I've connected with mental health organizations and received peer support from groups such as NAMI and This Is My Brave. I used my public relations skills to garner media coverage and booked over 30 speaking engagements. I became a part of This Is My Brave. I participated as a cast member first and seven months later, I co-produced a show with my castmate. It was the perfect opportunity to use all my skills to give others the opportunity to experience the freedom of sharing their truth.

Just when I thought school was behind me, I discovered the Certified Peer Recovery Specialist Certification by the Maryland Addiction and Behavioral Health Professionals Certification Board.

Some states call them peer counselors or consumer advocates, but the common theme is those with substance use or mental health disorders who are further along in their recovery supporting those who are just beginning their recovery, have recently relapsed, or just need additional support outside of their therapist and psychiatrist. Think of it as a life coach specifically for those with mental illness or a sponsor for those who struggled with alcohol abuse.

After being discharged from inpatient and partial hospitalization program, I felt lost and scared. I knew that I would be consistent in my treatment even though I was very fragile and unsure how my life would pan out. I felt alone, like an outcast and could not relate to anyone in my support system. There was no one in my circle who survived a suicide attempt or had the experience of being in the psychiatric unit. I tried to work but my mental illness got the best of me. I started to believe that I could not work, applied for disability, and thought that despite having two degrees from prestigious colleges, I would not be able to live a normal life.

I decided to become involved with my local NAMI chapter and participated in Peer-To-Peer Program, a class facilitated by people who live with a mental illness. The facilitators helped me develop a recovery plan and I connected with others who I could relate to. I said to myself, "Finally, people who get me," a judgement-free zone where I saw people with mental illness who worked full-time and lived productive lives. It gave me hope. The more I became involved with NAMI, the more I discovered that I could use my communications degrees to advocate for mental illness by educating my community. I decided to be what I needed earlier in my journey: a peer. So, I pursued a peer recovery specialist certification.

Research shows that peer support helps peer recovery specialists find purpose, advocate for self and others, increases empathy, encourages recovery and acceptance. In addition, it builds community, reduces hospital stays and stigmas, and promotes self-efficiency, according to the Substance Abuse and Mental Health Services Administration. I wish I had a "me" (peer recovery specialist) in my darkest days as it truly helps to have someone in your corner who understands.

I am pursuing my certification and paying for it out of pocket. I also find free trainings where I am able to obtain my continuing education credits (CEUs) and apply for scholarships. I am also one of the leads for a research project for a non-profit and mental health agency in Maryland.

The project examines the effects of enhanced peer support services and benefits counseling to individuals who receive vocation services and disability support from the government. The research program will compare the data from those who have a recovery peer support specialist (i.e. me), vocational services and clinical team versus those who only receive mental health treatment and vocation services.

I remember praying and asking God for an opportunity that would give me the flexibility to manage my mental health, have a work life balance, and remain self-employed. I got just that with the research project that I support. The opportunity also affords me the chance to write articles, develop communication strategies, and speak at conferences about my mental health recovery. Talk about an opportunity created just for me! I cannot take the credit; it was nobody but God.

Tatum of Blessed and Bossed Up says, "Say yes to your calling because someone's blessing is contingent upon your yes." I was recently appointed to serve on Maryland's Governor Commission on Suicide Prevention and the Behavioral Health Advisory Council. When I got the voicemail on my phone, I cried as I was thrilled for the honor. But, I experienced sadness too. I thought to myself, if I would have successfully ended my life, I would not be here to experience the wholeness I feel. Wholeness is every human's birthright. It is something that cannot be explained only experienced.

I remember what it was like walking around with a false sense of happiness, no peace, and broken to my core. The scripture reminds me that, "God heals the brokenhearted and binds up their wounds (Psalm 147:3), and "The Lord is near to the brokenhearted and saves those who are crushed in spirit (Psalm 34:18). I couldn't see it when I was in my dark days. Breann prayed with me on the phone; told me that what I was going through was for a reason and going to inspire others. I would roll my eyes and say, "Yeah, yeah." Now, I am the owner of Fireflies Unite, a mental health media and communications company with a mission to bring light into darkness (just like the fireflies) by sharing the stories of those who live and THRIVE with a mental illness in communities of color through its podcast, my speaking engagements, mental health events, books, forthcoming magazine, and documentary. Guess what? My sis, Breann, was right. While my mental health journey was the most difficult challenge in my life, I would not change it for anyone else's. God always knows exactly what He's doing.

I reached out to a few people who support the podcast and the Fireflies Unite movement, and here's what they had to say:

"T-Kea Blackman is a creative, entrepreneurial, business woman who I call sister. Her kind spirit, bubbly personality, and commitment to friendship are unmatched. During the past 10 years, I have watched T-Kea turn her darkest days and into a bright new future. She has educated me and countless others on the stigma of mental health in communities of color and has created a safe place to discuss these issues on her podcast, Fireflies Unite. T-Kea fosters conversations that breakdown myths and barriers of individuals living with a mental illness and encourages them to thrive! Above all, I admire T-Kea for her bravery in overcoming suicide, using her personal experiences to educate and inspire others. T-Kea Blackman is one to watch as she will be a top leader of our generation!" - **Breann B. (Los Angeles, CA)**

"I have so enjoyed getting to know Kea through her podcast Fireflies Unite. Her transparency and honest talk about mental health has empowered me to share my story! Her podcast Fireflies Unite is boldly breaking the stigma for people of color who often do not get help out of fear. Kea's recovery shows that you can not only live with mental illness, but THRIVE with it. Kea has shown me the power of speaking your truth. She is

honest, and real about the peaks and the valleys of her recovery. Also watching Kea manage a podcast, a business, and practice self-care has shown me that people with mental illness can be successful." - **Lauren H. (Norfolk, VA)**

"T-Kea's mental health journey has been inspiring to watch. It's forced me to deal and heal from my own issues. She has become a force to be reckoned with by narrating her own story and championing mental health and illness in the Black community. I truly believe that her work will break the stigma and change the perception of seeking help for mental illness." - **Karla G. (Chicago, IL)**

"Her openness is unmatched. Her pure conversations bring light to the truth. She works tirelessly to help others create new lifestyles and make mental health a priority in communities of color. One of a kind and compassionate, T-Kea's openness on mental health has influenced my life. I feel blessed to have witnessed her and seen her influence the lives of countless others." - **Kayla E. (Dallas, TX)**

"I met T-Kea during my sophomore year at Howard University. We clicked instantly due to her infectious personality and sense of humor. Some of my fondest memories of us are all centered around laughter, especially due to her jokes about my southern accent. Even though she was a few years ahead of me, she kept in

contact with me after she graduated. Because Kea and I had developed an open friendship where we could talk and laugh about anything, she began to confide in me about her battle with mental illness. Little did she know, this helped me too because I didn't know what to do or how to seek help with some of things that I had been dealing with. Although it had been years since I actually spoke with Kea, I kept up with her via social media. I am so proud to see her shattering barriers and stigmas about mental health in the black community. Kea and I recently reconnected and I was able to confide in her about my battle with anxiety. She was so quick to assist me and she answered questions before I could even ask them. Kea helped me locate a therapist, explore financing options for mental healthcare, and be an overall support system through my mental health journey. I can't thank her enough! If she wouldn't have taken the first step years ago, I wouldn't be able to do the same now. May God continue to bless her and all of her endeavors." - **Ambria M. (Austin, TX)**

I also asked therapists who I've been blessed to meet and work with in some capacity during my advocacy work and here's what they had to say:

"T-Kea is one of the best mental health advocates to grace this earth. Her life, her survival, her transparency, and her victory will be shown throughout this book. As a young adult

who never imagined being in the forefront in this capacity, she is literally changing the way the world (young and older) looks at mental health and emotional well-being. Her passion to educate is amazing and inspiring. Your life will be impacted tremendously from her story!" - **Sharon J. Lawrence, LCSW-C (Prince George's County, Maryland)**

"Sharing your mental health journey has been empowering to many because they can see themselves in you. They see you working and sharing your struggles. They see you connecting with people and sharing how you need time away. Your dedication to being transparent about the transitions in your health can help people understand that it may be scary and that's okay. It's okay to still choose yourself and do what is best for you." - **Jaynay Johnson, MFT (Philadelphia, PA)**

"T-Kea's transition from surviving to thriving with a mental illness is nothing less than inspirational. Her willingness to share that story — powerful. The impact on those who hear her story — transformational. This is a book about living life, escaping death, keeping the faith, and winning!" - **Dr. Anita Phillips (Baltimore, MD)**

When I read the responses, what do you think I did? Cried? You're right. I am beyond amazed at how God took my darkest days and turned them into Fireflies Unite. Dr. Anita Phillips said to me, "God doesn't leave any scraps behind," and I would have never thought this would be my new life. If you don't remember anything else from this book, it is my hope that you are open to receive mental health treatment whether you have a mental illness or not, heal from trauma, define success for yourself, and let go of any unrealistic timelines you may have placed   yourself on. Please give yourself permission and release the pressure of feeling as if you have to choose your faith over therapy or vice versa. Remember you can pray and see a therapist. Commit to your healing as your liberty, joy, and healing are on the other side.

Mental Health Resources

Therapy For Black Girls
Therapy For Black Girls is an online space dedicated to encouraging the mental wellness of Black women and girls founded by Dr. Joy Bradford Harden. So often the stigma surrounding mental health issues and therapy prevent Black women from taking the step of seeing a therapist. She developed the space to present mental health topics in a way that feels more accessible and relevant.
Website: www.therapyforblackgirls.com

Therapy For Black Men
Therapy For Black Men is a directory to help men of color in their search for a therapist founded by mental health professional Vladimire Calixte. Using the directory, men can search by therapist location and specialization. Searching by location, the results will include the therapists near you and will display their credentials, location, and the issues they treat.
Website: www.therapyforblackmen.org

NotOk App
NotOk App is a free digital panic button to get you immediate support via text, phone call, or GPS location when you're struggling to reach out, created by brother and sister, Charlie and Hannah Lucas.
Website: www.notokapp.com

National Alliance On Mental Illness
National Alliance On Mental Illness (NAMI) is the nation's largest grassroots mental health organization dedicated to building better lives for the millions of Americans affected by mental illness. The

organization offers peer and family support through its programs and has chapters throughout the United States. Website: www.nami.org

This Is My Brave

This Is My Brave is a non-profit and its mission is to end the stigma surrounding mental health issues by sharing personal stories of individuals living successful, full lives despite mental illness through live performances, its YouTube and Blog. Website: www.thisismybrave.org

Psychology Today

Psychology Today is a mental health magazine that offers resources to help you manage your mental health and you can visit the website to find a therapist in your area. Website: www.psychologytoday.com/us

Open Path Collective

A non-profit that serves clients who lack health insurance or whose health insurance doesn't provide adequate mental health benefits.
Website: www.openpathcollective.org

Talkspace

Talkspace is an online and mobile therapy company that affords individuals the opportunity to receive therapy from the comfort on their phone at affordable rates. Website: www.talkspace.com

Better Help

Better Help is an online portal that provides direct-to-consumer access to behavioral health services. The online counseling and therapy services are provided through web-based interaction as well as phone and text communication. Website: www.betterhelp.com

National Suicide Hotline

The National Suicide Prevention Lifeline is a United States-based suicide prevention network of 161 crisis centers that provides a 24/7, toll-free hotline available to anyone in suicidal crisis or emotional distress. You can reach someone at 1 (800) 273-8255.
Website: www.suicidepreventionlifeline.org

Crisis Text Line

Crisis Text Line is free, 24/7 support for those in crisis. Text 741741 from anywhere in the US to text with a trained Crisis Counselor. Crisis Text Line trains volunteers to support people in crisis.
Website: www.crisistextline.org

Fireflies Unite: Healthy Minds Facebook Group

The Fireflies Unite: Healthy Minds Facebook Group is an extension of the podcast and gives individuals the opportunity to connect, discuss topics in a safe place and find resources. T-Kea hosts monthly Facebook lives and interviews guests such as therapists and those who live with a mental illness to show those that therapy is okay and mental illness does not have a look. You can access the closed Facebook group by visiting www.facebook.com/firefliespod and click the 'visit group' button. Answer the questions and an administrator will approve you to join the group.

Fireflies Unite Podcast With Kea

Fireflies Unite with Kea is a weekly podcast from the perspective of those who live and thrive with a mental illness. The mission is to bring light into darkness (just like the fireflies) and to normalize the mental health conversation within communities of color. Visit http://firefliesunite.buzzsprout.com/ and listen to the podcast from the site. Or you can select your preferred listening platform. The podcast is available on Apple Podcasts, Soundcloud, Spotify, Stitcher and Google Play Music.

ACKNOWLEDGEMENTS

Thank you, God, for your strength and love that helped me overcome the most tumultuous times of my life. I never thought that my life would inspire so many, but I am grateful for every obstacle because you've given me the power to win every fight. I wish there were enough words to express my love to my amazing family. Thank you, Mommy, Grandma Diane, Auntie Roni, CJ, Sabri, Khalid, Amajuwan, Amadi, Zahiyah, Shyann, and Grandma Minnie.

Many of us have heard of the national program, Big Brother and Big Sister. Well, I was blessed with the best Big Sister ever, Tammi, who has been in my life since I was 11-years-old. You have been one of my biggest influences and helped shape the woman who I've become. Thank you for loving me, supporting me, attending every event from pageants to graduations and pouring into me. I am so blessed to have you in my life.

Chi Chi and Bria, thank you for being there during the most vulnerable time of my life. I was so confused, angry, and lost. You were the first two people I saw after I was released from the hospital for my suicide attempt. Thank you for being there.

Where do I begin with my girl, Destiny? Destiny, thank you for everything that you've done for me from providing me with a listening ear, money when I needed it, prayers, attending my speaking engagements, telling me when I'm wrong and right; but, more importantly never leaving my side. I thank God for placing you in my life.

Bre Bre, my big sis from HU (the REAL HU, Destiny, LOL). We have been through so much together. Through it all, our relationship in God has kept us together. Thank you for the mornings you've answered my calls at 5 a.m. to pray for me and to let me cry. You were not one of those people who only said, "I am praying for you." You would stop what you were doing to pray with me over the phone. We've grown together in our mental health journey. I love you, girl.

Jazzy boo, thanks for the many laughs as I can always count on you to keep me in great spirits. Thank you for having my back especially when I was first diagnosed. You were one of the first people I told, and I did not feel judged, but supported. You know I love you girl!

I can't write a book about my mental health recovery and not thank the person who has been vital in my progress, Dr. Tucker. You've been my therapist for three and half years and I've made so much progress. You've gone above and beyond what most therapists would do from seeing me when I did not have insurance and could not afford my copay to sponsoring my first event to raise awareness for suicide among children of color. I've developed healthy coping strategies and learned to live life on my terms with your support. Thank you for everything, Dr. Tucker!

To my high school guidance counselor who I still talk to this day, Mr. O! Thank you for believing in me and supporting me during those times in high school where I struggled academically and became so consumed by trauma. You encouraged me to keep going and reminded me of my value.

To the McCreary Family, thank you for opening your home, going above and beyond by taking me in as your own. I will forever be grateful for your love and support. You did what some could not do and there are truly no words to express my appreciation, but I thank you for providing me with a space to recover.

Camommy and Cadaddy a.k.a Quamiece and Aaron, thank you for opening your own home and supporting me. I love you dearly and appreciate everything you've done.

To my Aunt Tut, who is no longer with me on earth, but in my heart. Thank you for your love and support throughout the years. I know you may not have understood everything, but your presence and love means more than you know.

A special thank you to Jennifer Marshall and my This Is My Brave family for providing me a safe space to share my story and connect with others.

Last but certainly not least, thank you to my Fireflies Unite family which includes every person who listens to the podcast or has been a guest, attended a speaking engagement, sponsored one of my events, and purchased this book. I do not take any of your support for granted.

References:

Mental Health Gov:
www.mentalhealth.gov/basics/what-is-mental- health

The National Alliance on Mental Illness:
www.nami.org

Childhood Domestic Violence Association
https://cdv.org/2014/02/10-startling-domestic-violence-statistics-for-children/

Strange Fruit And Spanish Moss Blog:
http://strangefruitandspanishmoss.blogspot.com/2014/10/october-8-1926-clarence-demon-and.html

Black Then:
https://blackthen.com/one-south-carolinas-tragic-horrific-family-lynchings/

Aiken Standard:
www.aikenstandard.com/news/sheriff-howard- was-last-officer-killed-by-gunshot-in-aiken/article_761204c0-95ad-5b92-8855-d98fa8f747e7.html

The Association of Child and Adolescent Mental Health:
www.acamh.org/blog/intergenerational-trauma/
Ayalon, L., & Young, M. A. (2005). Racial group differences in help-seeking behaviors. The Journal of Social Psychology, 145, 391–403.
doi:10.3200/SOCP.145.4.391-404

Bell-Tolliver, L., & Wilkerson, P. (2011). The use of spirituality and kinship as contributors to successful therapy outcomes with African American families. Journal of Religion & Spirituality in Social Work: Social Thought, 30, 48–70. doi:10.1080/15426432.2011.542723

DuBois, W. E. B. (Ed.). (1903). The negro church. Walnut Creek, CA: Altamira Press.

Johnson, M. V. (2010). The tragic vision of African American religion. New York, NY: Palgrave MacMillan.

Lincoln, C. E., & Mamiya, L. H. (1990). The Black Church in the African American experience. Durham, NC: Duke University Press.

Pew Research Center. (2009, January). A religious portrait of African-Americans: www.pewforum.org/2009/01/30/a-religious-portrait-of-african-americans/

Whitley, R. (2012). "Thank you God:" Religion and recovery from dual diagnosis among low-income African Americans. Transcultural Psychiatry, 49, 87–104. doi:10.1177/1363461511425099

Wilmore, G. S. (1998). Black religion and black radicalism: An interpretation of the religious history of African Americans (3rd ed.). Maryknoll, NY: Orbis Books.

The Professional Counselors. The Black Church: Theology and Implications for Counseling African Americans: http://tpcjournal.nbcc.org/the-black-church-theology-and-implications-for-counseling-african-americans

Livestrong:
www.livestrong.com/article/456698-can- starving-yourself-lead-to-weight-gain-when-you-return- to-normal-eating-habits/

Healthline:
www.healthline.com/health/depression/exercise #1

Substance Abuse Mental Health Services Administration (SAMHSA):
www.samhsa.gov/capt/applying-strategic-prevention/cultural-competence

About the Author

T-Kea Blackman, MPS (also known as Kea) is a mental health advocate, speaker, and author. She is the creator and host of the Fireflies Unite Podcast, a weekly podcast dedicated to bringing light into darkness (just like the fireflies) by sharing the stories of individuals thriving with mental illness within communities of color despite the disadvantages and racism that negatively impact their mental health.

Described as an inspiration, her heartfelt and powerful story is a testament that anyone can thrive despite having a mental illness. T-Kea was diagnosed with major depression and generalized anxiety disorders and is a suicide survivor. She previously worked in the television industry as a publicist and production/talent coordinator. Within her career, she provided support to TV One's signature award-winning shows Unsung and Unsung Hollywood, BET's Black Girls Rock!, The Soul Train Awards and BET X Youth Experience. Her diagnosis led her to use her communications and media skills to raise awareness for mental illness within communities of color.

As a peer recovery coach for a mental health research project in the state of Maryland, T-Kea provides peer support to clients with mental illness and intellectual disabilities where she uses her real experience with mental illness to assist clients with their personal and professional goals. She is currently pursuing her certification through the Maryland and Behavioral Health Professional Certification Board to become a certified recovery coach/peer recovery specialist. She is a certified Wellness Recovery Action Plan (WRAP®)

Trainer where she facilitates training to those who want to make their mental and emotional health a priority. WRAP® is a personalized recovery system of wellness tools and action plans to achieve a self-directed wellness vision despite life's daily challenges.

T-Kea's articles have been published on The Mighty, Urban Faith, Blavity, and 21 Ninety. Making a digital footprint, her articles have garnered over 50,000 views and encouraged individuals to seek treatment. T-Kea wrote her first book, Saved & Depression: A Suicide Survivor's Journey Of Mental Health, Healing, & Faith to educate her community on mental health also encouraging them to seek treatment.

In April 2018, T-Kea was appointed by the Governor's office to serve on Maryland's Behavioral Health Advisory Council. In Spring 2018, T-Kea participated as a cast member for This Is My Brave: Arlington Show, a storytelling show for those with mental and/or substance use disorders and went on to co-produce the fall Arlington Show.

She serves as an In Our Own Voice program leader for the National Alliance on Mental Illness (NAMI), the nation's largest grassroots mental health organization dedicated to building better lives for the millions of Americans affected by mental illness.

She earned a master's degree in public relations and corporate communications from Georgetown University, and a bachelor's degree in radio, television and film production from Howard University.

To follow T-Kea's journey and listen to her podcast, visit www.firefliesunite.com and connect with her @firefliespod on Facebook, Twitter, and Instagram.

CPSIA information can be obtained
at www.ICGtesting.com
Printed in the USA
LVHW041514100919
630593LV00010B/940/P